✠ this we believe

MEDITATIONS ON THE APOSTLES' CREED

JOHN A. ROSS

ⓐABINGDON PRESS • NASHVILLE • NEW YORK

✠
Preface

This is my first book. I never really intended to write a book at all. DeCourcy H. Rayner, the editor of *The Presbyterian Record,* asked me to write a series of articles for him on the Apostles' Creed. "Something different," he said, "something a layman can read." I think he expected me to send in six short articles. He must have been dismayed when he saw that my six articles had covered only the first clause in the Creed! I was uncovering whole mines of meaning under each of the ancient words, and my delight was ever so much stronger than my editorial discretion. Mr. Rayner graciously extended the series until it had run its natural course. Month by month I wrestled with profound theological issues until I could say what I believed in a few simple words. Clause by clause, word by word, I pressed on, forced to say something about everything. I was unable to avoid any of those unpopular phrases about which few people have much good to say. If I had not been compelled to consider all of those subjects carefully, I might have bypassed them rather lightly. Yet often I discovered that neglecting these phrases has deprived many of us of the satisfaction of possessing a complete panorama of faith.

Many of the letters which came to me during the run of the articles expressed the hope that they would be reprinted soon in the form of a book. I could not easily discount so much encouragement from ministers, laymen, church school teachers, overseas missionaries, and university students. *The Presbyterian Record* was willing to republish anything from the original articles. Some inquiries brought forth the suggestion that recasting them into a devotional format would make the material useful to even more readers. So I reworked the original articles to meet new requirements, and here is the book that I never intended to write.

A word is in order about the title *This We Believe*. Readers may think it strange to have "We" in the title and so very much of "I" in the book. There isn't much theology written these days in the first person singular.

But the Creed of the church says *"I* believe," and it seemed appropriate that I should do likewise. No church, of course, is to be held responsible for any of the unusual twists I may have given to common Christian doctrines, but "We" and "I" are so entirely intertwined in my mind that either word would be appropriate. In any case, I hope that when a reader comes to the word "I," he will read *himself* into it and make the thoughts his own. Then it will really be what *We* believe, and the title will be justified.

These days the most-talked-about religious books all express an uneasy discontent with old beliefs. Too few of them are making positive contributions toward the reconstruction of faith in our times. It was good discipline for me to set myself the task of writing out what I believe in *positive,* rather than negative terms.

The study of theology is not often conducted in a devotional spirit, and I was pleased to see that this can be done. Also I have noticed that all too much theological writing about creeds and confessions of faith has little to do with Christ who, after all, ought to be at the very center of all the ideas which can properly be called Christian. It gave me great satisfaction to set all my thoughts on the Creed in formation around Jesus Christ. This manoeuvre must be performed by any future reformation of theology if it is to stand the test of time. My book sets out to be something of a "Christique" of the Creed. As such it could be part of the basis for a new style of Christian approach to the post-modern world.

7

I am truly grateful to my wife Kay and to my son Robin for all their help in test-reading and discussing various drafts of the manuscript. Behind the scenes always was my faithful secretary, Elsie Carson, patiently typing and retyping. The collaboration of the four of us makes the book's title appropriate: This *We* Believe.

JOHN A. ROSS.

Vancouver, British Columbia.

The Apostles' Creed

I believe in God the Father almighty,
maker of heaven and earth;

and in Jesus Christ his only Son, our Lord;
who was conceived by the Holy Ghost,
born of the Virgin Mary,
suffered under Pontius Pilate,
was crucified, dead, and buried;
he descended into hell;
the third day he rose again from the dead;
he ascended into heaven,
and sitteth on the right hand of God the Father
almighty;
from thence he shall come to judge the quick and
the dead.

I believe in the Holy Ghost;
the holy catholic church;
the communion of saints;
the forgiveness of sins;
the resurrection of the body;
and the life everlasting.

Amen.

The Apostles' Creed

When I stand shoulder to shoulder with Christians, all declaring our common faith in the words of the Apostles' Creed, something very deep stirs within me. I feel like a tree out in the great forest, surrounded by other trees all reaching up together from the same ground, all swept by the same wind, all steadily voicing the same ageless sounds that swaying trees have always made. Long long ago, those about to be received into the Church affirmed their faith even as we do now. Wherever people meet in the name of Christ throughout the world, the Apostles' Creed, like the Lord's Prayer, is quite in order. This creed joins me to the whole Church up through the centuries and across the continents and seas. It expresses what Jesus Christ means to us all. This is the place where I meet my brothers in the Lord, even though we sometimes draw apart again all too soon. Although the legend is not true that each of the twelve apostles contributed one doctrine to make up the whole Apostles' Creed, they would undoubtedly all have approved of this common core of faith.

The word "creed" comes from the Latin word "credo," which means "I believe." When I say the creed I hold my head high, and my voice sounds out, firm and strong. This is indeed what I believe about the one in whom I believe. As a man of the twentieth century, I don't mumble the creed with mental reservations or leave out an occasional phrase. I'm always finding new significance for Jesus Christ in every word of it. It contains in outline form the whole message which the Church has to give to the world. It says at one burst what I want to tell everybody everywhere. I'm excited about this. It's what I believe. It makes sense of the world and it gives meaning to my life. It makes my heart sing and I want to share it all.

I must not shrink from speaking up about the things that could save our times from their stumbling futility. There's no scarcity of bad news about the world these days, but who's got some good news? Well, I, for one, have some! If the creed is right—if I do know the one to whom this world really belongs and know how he intends it to run, and that he has made adequate resources available for making the best-dreams-ever come true—I should speak up and say, "This I believe!" Dare I keep still while lives are going to pieces all around me? What sinister enemy so gags me that I can't faithfully say the name of Jesus or express my trust in him in front of other people? When I join publicly in the creed, I defy that enemy. Really, though, it's not too hard to speak out in Church where I have the safety of numbers. But does my faith lose its voice outside the Church? The Church is not in the world to be forever talking to itself. Its good news is for the whole world. Its creed is a creed for the whole world. No congregation can be fully sincere in merely reciting it without making some personal effort to pass it along to those unhappy mixed-up people who are all around us. The Apostles' Creed is a creed for apostles—those whom Christ sends out.

I believe . . .

What I believe is very important, for one belief is not as good as another. If I grope my way in the dark to the medicine cabinet and take poison pills, believing them to be good for me, it's disastrous! My utmost sincerity won't save me. All accidents, failures, mistakes, and sins stem from faulty beliefs. Nobody can be one hundred percent certain about what to believe in most situations. I know so very little about this complicated, changing world. I just haven't got time to obtain *perfect knowledge* about things before I act. I couldn't possibly check over every detail about an aircraft, its crew, the weather, the airports, and other plane positions before going on board for a flight. I can only believe that someone entirely unknown to me has checked on everything. In fact, I must live every moment of every day in faith as everybody else does. There is no other way I can live. I have to get by on *believing* because I can never *know* for sure. This is especially true of my view of the world as a whole. Where do I fit into the scheme of things? What am I here for? What is expected of me? What will become of me? This kind of big question can be answered for me only by religious beliefs.

But what religious beliefs should I have? I certainly can't be satisfied with explanations of the world which never rise to the level of some great personal purpose. But in whose purpose shall I believe? I'm used to believing experts, eyewitnesses, and properly accredited authorities. I need to find some acknowledged expert on living, someone men have really seen in action, whose way of life and beliefs were backed up by the highest known authority.

On this basis, I believe in Jesus of Nazareth. He was a real, historical man, whose sayings and deeds were endorsed by no less than the very power behind this universe. This world will not back up falsity and lies. Truth and reality go together. Unlike all other men who ever lived, this man's life was not allowed to stay dead forever. Within three days he rose from the dead. The power that can defeat death so decisively must be the greatest power there is. This greatest of all authorities sustained Jesus through death. His life of loyalty to truth, his incomparable compassion obviously satisfied God—the first man who ever did so. I can base my ultimate faith, therefore, on this unique man who lives forever. Because I believe in him, I know what to believe. I can believe in what Jesus believed and said and did. Jesus believed and taught that *he* was what God had to say about men's ultimate questions. So I believe that Jesus is my clue to the meaning of all things.

Now I know who I am. I am one who believes in the God who shines through Jesus. I belong to him. As a strangely shaped bar of metal takes on meaning only when it becomes a tool in the hands of a workman, so I get my meaning from the God who has me at his disposal. His purpose, declared in Jesus, is my purpose. The lives of wandering, purposeless men can take on deep meaning and significance when they are put back into the hands of God, where they always belonged.

I believe in God . . .

No matter how many good reasons I might give for believing in the God I see in Christ, none of these can compel anyone else to believe in him. To tell the truth, I didn't really come to my belief by a lot of close observations and hard thinking. I can't take any credit for my believing, as if it were my own good work. I suspect that something of Christ got into me and that he is, in me, believing in himself. The hidden God hides himself in the people of his true church. We simply discover this miracle that he has worked in us. My believing is more his work than mine. But now that I do believe in him, I can see that my belief is quite sensible and that it makes sense of everything. My belief also gives me a program for living constructively. Its value can be judged only by the last word that will be spoken about it by the highest authority at the end of history. In the meantime, lacking anyone to surpass Jesus in mastering both life and death, I have decided to stick with him. I have put myself and my deepest concerns trustfully in his hands. All my weight is resting upon this God. I believe that he is able to uphold me through everything. Because I believe in God, I shall come to know more about God. When I believe enough in a surgeon, I will allow him to cut me open under anesthetic when I'm unconscious and helpless. Then I come to know something about his skill, about my own condition, and perhaps about what new health is like. Because I believed in God first, I have come to believe the Creed.

I probably shouldn't expect anyone else to believe the

Creed unless they think well of the way I and my fellow believers live. What a man really believes is shown through his actions. My life story will illustrate what my creed really is. A man's beliefs are the most important thing about him. If a prospective son-in-law believes that the world owes him a living, the girl's father had better have a little chat with his daughter! So when I say that I believe in God, I don't mean that this is merely my go-to-church-and-say-my-Sunday-prayers frame of mind. It's got to make a difference at my office tomorrow because I believe in God. My wife and family must not be worrying about what I'm doing when I'm out of their sight. I must watch how I spend my life's time and money because I believe in God. Since my faith affects all of me, it will affect everything I touch. My point of view, my reactions, my decisions, all will be influenced by the fact that I believe in God. Well, lots of them are. But again and again I somehow get a wild idea that I can run my life in some way other than Christ's way. That spells trouble because my life strangely insists on being run according to Christ's way or else it kicks back at me. I just hope that when I fail to live my normal faith, the tragic cost of my failure will prove, in a left-handed way, that my normal faith is quite right. Whether I practice what I profess or not, I have to come back to belief in God. His rebuke convinces me as much as his blessing. Even the man who believes in unbelief finds out a lot about God's ways sooner or later, whether he likes them or not.

17

I believe in God ...

The dignity of God doesn't depend on what I think of him. Any crown he wears wasn't placed there by me or any other man. Jesus' rank was not conferred upon him by councils of people like me. God himself pronounced Jesus to be utterly worthy of living forever, wielding all the power there is. That's what Christ's resurrection implies. Many men of those times who had been quite sure that God couldn't become man and that God couldn't raise the dead felt that they now had to speak of the risen Jesus as "my Lord and my God!" This solitary figure who fought his way back from the depths of death must have been either God himself, the creator of life, or one of the same kind. Jesus' resurrection terribly upset people's ideas about God. Were there actually *two* Gods? To make matters worse, when some of Jesus' disciples were praying together at Pentecost, they felt themselves caught up by the same power that had carried Jesus along. Christ's own spirit (ghost) was now living and working in *them!* Somehow they had become a new earthly body for Christ. This meant that the one God of their fathers had a *threeness* about him! According to their experience, the one God was Father, Son, Holy Ghost —three living elements working together in perfect unity. The disciples couldn't even tell people what had happened to them and what God they were talking about, without using expressions which implied the tri-unity, the trinity of God. But can three ones be one, or three and one be the same? The Jews said that such talk was blasphemy. Yet the early Christians simply couldn't account for themselves apart from a God who had possessed them in three ways: as Almighty Creator, as victorious Savior, and as activating Spirit. The threeness of the one God accounted for the three parts of the one story that Christians had to tell: the Father's eternal plan to bring men to himself, his Son's coming to make it possible, and his Spirit's working to bring it to pass. The truth of the trinity of God was at the heart of the gospel. If God had not become man in Christ, then the great gap between the Holy God and his sinful creatures in this world would not have been overcome. Then there would still not be any reasonable hope of final victory over sin and death. We would be cut off, isolated on an island of despair and death without bridge or boat.

The trinitarian formula of the Creed is the only one that takes into account all facts about Jesus and his apostles, and makes sense of them. Any other way of expressing God always eliminates something important from the New Testament, explains it away, drastically reinterprets it, plays it down, or mutilates it somehow. Any gods I may dream up must be squared with the experience of the first Christians. The Creed reminds me that from the earliest days it was not possible for a Christian to believe anything whatsoever he happened

19

to fancy. I believe in the Father Almighty . . . his only Son . . . the Holy Ghost—the God of the Creed.

I believe in God . . .

Although I believe in God, that doesn't mean that I know everything about him. It used to bother me when people asked me big questions about God that I couldn't answer. Now I'm glad that I couldn't answer them. Any god I could know everything about would be far too small to be the real God. Would the Arctic Ocean fit inside my refrigerator? Could I capture a great storm in a gallon jug? Can I get the Creator of all the world inside my little skull? But although I don't know everything about God, in Christ I know enough about him to get started. He is what I see in Jesus Christ, and who knows how much more? I don't understand the Trinity, nor does anybody else. I don't understand how God could become man, nor does anybody else. But if God is like Christ, that makes sense of the world and helps me to understand a great deal about my meaning and destiny.

There are lots of things I don't understand about the way God made the world and about the way he is running it. Sometimes I have tried to think up a better world than this one. I object to the inequalities I see among men—but then I wouldn't want to be absolutely identical with everyone else. How confusing it would be! Sometimes God is criticized for allowing things and people we love to pass away. But I don't think I would like an unchanging world, without possibilities for newness in it, although all changes do away with something that once was. Sometimes I think that God should interfere promptly and stop people who are about to hurt others. But that would turn us persons into machines, and I fear God would be switching us off most of the time! Sometimes I wish that water wouldn't drown, or fire wouldn't burn, or falling wouldn't hurt. But unless the things in the world behave themselves consistently according to their natures, the world would be all helter-skelter. I'd be driven crazy! I'd certainly like to get along without pain, but how would I find out about threats to my body if there were never any pain warnings? Any worlds that I ever dream up would be far worse to live in than this one God made. So I believe in God in spite of everything that seems to contradict my faith. I wish I could believe in myself with as great confidence as I can believe in him! I can never be sure that I will always be faithful and never fall away. Probably I shall never in this world reach a state of uninterrupted believing. But I believe that I shall always be held in the midst of the unbroken faithfulness of God. Even though my faith may waver, falter, or fail, my God will not waver, falter, or fail. Though I forget him, he will not forget me. If I should not even feel religious tomorrow, his feeling for me would not change. Even if my mind should blow a fuse and go dark, though I should faint, sleep, or utterly die, *I believe in God.*

I believe in God . . .

The Apostles' Creed has lasted throughout the centuries because God has always been the creed's kind of God, and because Christians have always been going through the same experiences as the first Christians who set up the Creed. God has always been the creator, the only true creator, and he always will be creator. He didn't become Father for the first time the day Jesus was born. The Son of God came into this world from the depths of the eternal Father. The Holy Ghost did not come into existence when Jesus left this earthly scene. It was by his Holy Spirit that God first created the worlds for purposes enwrapped in his Son. Because God has always been and always will be Father, Son, Holy Ghost, I know that he will not change his mind toward his world. His Word in the Christ of the Creed will never become false or outmoded. His last word about the universe will be the same as his first word. Man-made gods may come and go. They are as fickle as human fancies. But this eternal God, whom I know through Jesus, enables me to go about my business, living with a good deal of joyful confidence. I know how things are. I know what to expect.

That's why I'm not surprised that the same kinds of things that happened to New Testament Christians can also happen to people today, even to me. The Word of Christ which remained with us after he disappeared as a bodily presence has been operating in his church and world ever since. This same Word has been implanted in me like a seed of Christ by faithful parents, friends, and servants of the Lord. The ageless Creator Spirit is at work with that Word, growing something of Christ in me day by day, shaping up in me something of Christ's compassion and love for reality. He rebukes me and stretches me, subtracting here and adding there. Somehow I can say that Christ really dwells in my heart. Under these circumstances I've just got to believe in the Father God, because the Spirit of his Son keeps reaching out to him from within me. I must acknowledge Christ as the Son of God because I know that it is Christ's Spirit in me that has set my no-good heart a-yearning for his Father and home. Who could convince me that his Spirit has not done this? Who else could turn my life on, as he has?

Wherever the Word of Christ has gone throughout the centuries, Christians have appeared. In making Christians, the God of the Creed proves himself. The outgoing God who so loved men that he laid aside his own glory and came into the thick of human life still goes out to all men through me and his church. The Creed's story is relevant to the whole human race. All men are creatures of a fatherly kind of God. All men wrestle with the same kind of human nature that was worn by God the Son. The Spirit of truth and love is a healing power for everyone. The Creed of the Trinity is indeed a Creed for apostles: men sent out by God to the whole world.

... the Father ...

When Jesus of Nazareth addressed the almighty Creator of the universe as "Father," he said what he meant and meant what he said. Pagans were always inventing tales about gods with their families of godlings. Sometimes poets dreamed that some men were somehow divine offspring. The prophets of Israel believed that a God who loved them "like a father" would rescue them. But when Jesus called upon his Father, he was not using a figure of speech or stretching his imagination. He had really come from the Lord God as life springs from life. Father and Son were of the same kind. A ventriloquist's dummy might call his maker "father," but nevertheless the dummy and his maker are not of the same kind. I and other men are merely God's creatures. We are not his kind. We could never properly be called God's sons unless the Spirit of his only Son came to dwell in us. But with the Son-

Spirit in me, I *may* call God "my Father" and mean exactly that. "To all who received him he gave power to become children of God," says the gospel. I believe that this wondrous possibility has really come to pass in me because I find in me something that holds out arms to the Father and yearns for him and strives to please him. I am a son of God! Imagine that! Whenever I have met others who believe that God is their Father in this way, they and I have known a strange thrill of brotherhood and an unspoken understanding that is quite unmistakable. When we Christians first realize that God the Creator has become also our Father, we don't know whether we should shout our joy all over his world, or whether we should be stricken dumb with amazement that it should be so!

At night when I look up at the sweep of the stars that God has made, I can say with pride: "All those belong to my Father." When I deal with this world's creatures all around me, I must treat them with dignity and respect. They all belong to my Father and not to me. I am responsible to him for the way I handle them. When I look upon the teeming millions of stumbling wanderers in the world who don't know who they are or what they are here for, I feel I must tell them, "You belong to my Father." I must share my Father's Word and world with them. When there are others who in truth call God their Father through Christ, I must recognize that they are my brothers, fellow sons of the Father. The real church is the real family of the eternal Father. My belief in God the Father makes a big dif-

25

ference in my life. It pulls my world together and holds us all together.

... the Father ...

If I believe in my Father I must behave like a child of the Father. I must be childlike in the best sense, but not childish. I must recognize how dependent I am upon my Father and trust him to arrange things to provide for my needs. I may not know what my Father does in his office, but he knows what he is doing and it is good. I may forget him in the rush of many things, but he will not forget me. He may be very busy, but he always has time for me and a special place for me in his heart and plans. When I suffer, he suffers. My problems are his problems. I am his problem —his problem child. He has so much to teach me, and he leads me to wisdom by the experiences through which I come. Nothing ever merely *happens* to me. My Father has his eye on everything. He knows what is going on and why. Whatever men may do, this world is not going to career and smash its way to utter disaster until my Father is finished with it. My Father is at the wheel, so I can sleep at night. I know my Father will not go to sleep.

Because I believe in my Father I feel a responsibility for maintaining the dignity of his name, our family's name. I must never, never let him down! He expects me to be at my best for his name's sake. Think of all he has done for me: He gave me my life and everything that I have; he took me into his family and called me his. If I should be cold toward him, or cruel toward his creatures, I would bring deep disgrace on his heart of love. If I should be ungrateful, negligent, unfaithful, a fake, or a liar, what would this do to him? Another cross? If I am truly his son, people ought to be able to see in me some family resemblance. If I should take his name on me in vain, this would be the ultimate profanity.

I believe that God will always be my Father. Even if I dishonor him, he will not cut me off forever. When I come back to my senses and remember whose son I am, he'll be ready for me with open arms. That kind of love can be neither defeated nor forgotten. I wonder why he would love the likes of me? I haven't anything to give him that he didn't first give to me except, possibly, my love for him. But maybe he gave me that too. The love with which his only begotten Son always loved him still loves him through me. Why does he love me? Just because he is Love. He is the Father.

. . . the Father . . .

I have taught my children to pray to "our Father in heaven." When they hear God called "Father," do they think about their earthly father and wonder if God is like me? Some children hate the very sound of the word "father" because it reminds them of a man who played the fool in their family and blighted their lives. In my children's understanding of their heavenly Father, may I be a window, not a closed door.

God's fatherhood is very different from mine, indeed his is quite unique. There was a time when I was not a father. But God the Father and God the Son have always been together. By myself, without a mate, I could never have been a father. But God is Father in himself. My children came into being through an unbelievable, complicated process with which I had little to do. But God the Father was entirely and always involved in the being of his Son. I can't really understand the fatherhood of God by considering merely my own fatherhood. It seems that there are two kinds of fatherhood, and that's that. My fatherhood after the flesh is only a very pale shadow of that of God. My name as father is derived from his reality as the eternal Father of the eternal Son, not the other way around.

Perhaps I am only truly and wholly a father when I have spiritual children. Almost any man can become a biological father. But unmarried people like Paul found that they could father spiritual sons such as Timothy. How can this be? Because the Spirit of the Son is the same as the Spirit of the Father. If this Spirit is in me, I can not only be a son of God but also a god*father* to some other person. When the Word of Christ which is in me has been passed along to some other person, the Spirit of God can use that Word for a new start in that other life. Thus somebody else can become my son in the spirit as well as a son of God. When my children-after-the-flesh become my children-in-the-Spirit, then I have become their father in a deeper sense than ever before. Even unmarried people can become parents in the Lord. Thank God for parents who gave us birth, and thank God for parents in the Lord. Blessed are they for whom these two sets of parents are one and the same. These children will find it easy to believe in God the Father.

. . . the Father . . .

I believe in the Father. I wouldn't like to call him "Pop!" He's somewhat above hot dogs and baseball games. I wouldn't like to call him "Daddy," for he's beyond coaxing, or "Dad," for he's not a bit out of touch with what's new. Nor is he "Grandpa"! I'd better not expect God to slip me any illicit favors or privileges. My Father knows what's good for me and part of his love for me is shown by the way he brings me back to be what I ought to be, and to do what I ought to do. He disciplines me, and that's one way by which I know he cares about me. He knows what he wants me to be and I have to learn what he considers to be important and valuable. There's no use arguing

with him about these things. My Father is the Lord
God, the Creator of all that is.

How can it be that the Lord God would stoop low
and tenderly say to me, "My son"? How can it be that
such a one would take such infinite pains to bring me
up? O Father! My Father! What a shame people think
of you as a mere cosmic force, the great reasoning
machine, the big push who set the universe in motion.
You are Father—personal as your Son was personal.
Like Father, like Son. I as your son, too, must be careful to love people as persons and not treat them merely
as things I can use.

Jesus came into conflict with men because he said
God was his Father, and because his Father's plan for
men cut right across his people's whole way of life.
Face to face with the prospect of dying a horrible death,
he had to choose between being loyal to his Father and
escaping from a cross. In the Garden of Gethsemane
Jesus sweated it out: "My Father, if it be possible, let
this cup pass from me; nevertheless, not as I will, but
as thou wilt." I wonder if, when my turn comes to
choose between my loyalty to my Father in heaven and
my continuance in comfortable living, *I* shall be able
to say, "The cup which my Father hath given to me,
shall I not drink it?" Or shall I turn in anger against
the God who let me get into such a horrible predica-
ment? God, grant that *I* shall be able to feel and say
from my heart, "Father, forgive them." Whatever I
may be called upon someday to suffer, at the end may

I be able to fall asleep in my Father's arms saying, "Father, into thy hands I commit my spirit."

Come what may, this is my Father's world. Wherever I go, I am only moving about in his house. Someday I'll be leaving this old world that I have known and loved for so long. People will say I am dead. But don't believe them. I have just gone down the long hallway to another room in my Father's house to have a look at some of his best treasures.

. . . almighty

In all ages the people of God have been laughed to scorn and harassed to death. Yet in their distress they were upheld by believing in the Almighty God. Their faith in God's final victory over all their enemies gave them the hope and the courage to sing even in their darkest hours. Christians knew that men had done their very worst to the Son of the Almighty upon the cross, but that nevertheless Christ had risen from the dead, showing himself to be Lord of all. With such a Savior and such a Father they could lift up their hearts. So the faithful, though victims, may still rejoice, for the Lord God Omnipotent reigns!

I believe in the Almighty. All my powers come from him, even my ability to believe in him. By myself I am utterly weak. Every move I make depends on food that I did not make. I require so many things to keep on living that I spend most of my life trying to gather them together. But the Almighty does not have to strain and struggle for dear life. At the end of my day I am at the end of my energy and I drop off to sleep. The Almighty, however, does not nod upon his throne. I can change things around in my household, in my office, and sometimes in my neighborhood or town. But beyond that my powers have little effect. The arm of the Almighty reaches to the ends of the earth and to the end of all ends. A small cord is quite sufficient to tie me up, but a cable as great as the Milky Way could not bind the Almighty. A tiny bullet can finish me off, but the explosion of ten thousand suns is all in a day's work for him. I can only look upon the outside of things that are near me. The Almighty is always looking right into the core of everything everywhere. There is no hiding from him. Nor will he ever lose or mislay me.

I believe that the Almighty is also the All-Good because it was Christ whom he raised up from the dead. He honored the best that has ever been. I'm glad that the All-Good, the Almighty, has chosen to be a Father to me. Suppose he were like a great cat and I a little mouse in his grasp. If the one with all the power were also the All-Wicked . . . ! If the Almighty were even such a one as I am, what a nightmare the world would become! Yet sometimes I forget what I am and almost presume to tell the Almighty how he ought to be running his world. I'm glad I don't have all the responsi-

bility he carries. The world should be glad of it, too!
Sometimes I get so tired of the stream of telephone
calls and appointments. When I'm worn out by pleas
and clamoring needs, I long for a day off, a holiday.
But the Almighty never gets a day off. When it's
quitting time for God, that will be the finale of everything.

. . . almighty

God is all-*might*-y. The word "might" has two
meanings: It either expresses the *possibility* that something may happen, or it refers to the *power* that can
bring to pass what is possible. God's might shares in
both meanings. Before the worlds began, God decided
what he would do and permit, as well as what he would
not do or permit, in his creation. This great decision
fixed forever what is possible in this world (what might
come into being) and what is impossible (what cannot
ever successfully come to pass). The Almighty's primal
decree laid down the constitution of the universe and
settled forever the nature of things and men. Anything
which the Almighty created may operate only within the
limits of the possibilities which God's law has set for it.
God has also the might, the power, to do all that may
be done, all that is possible according to his law. He
can control what he has created, uphold and preserve

it or, if necessary, let it go back down again to nothing when it has served its purpose. He is all-might-y. He has no ultimate rivals to stand over him. The same God who gave the Word that created the worlds will have the last Word about their destiny too. The Father of our Lord Jesus Christ is the source of all authority, ability, and reality.

If all might belongs to him, am I then only a helpless toy in his hands? I certainly seem to move at my own commands. But if I always have to do what he makes me do, it would be hard for me to explain all my mistakes and sins. Then God would have to bear the blame for all the crimes of the human race. If my children were not free to rage against me, their freely given love would mean nothing to me. Even the Almighty would not likely rejoice when, at the push of a button, he heard a talking toyman say, "I love you." When I hear him command "thou shalt . . ." or "thou shalt not . . ." I believe he assumes that it is up to me to decide whether or not I am going to obey him. Within limits I can do what I want to do when I want to do it. The Almighty sets obvious bounds to my freedom but, inside my "cage," I am free to be what I am. I can choose how I shall react to anything that happens to me. To a large degree I am therefore responsible for the direction my life takes. When I try to be what I am not, to live in a way not permitted to me by God, then I am destroying myself either slowly or suddenly. What is outlawed by God always contains within itself the means of its own destruction. But

Jesus is the indestructible One,—God's Way, Truth, and Life. He is the true way for man to live. He is the way for man to live truly. His truth will make me free. But when I go against his way of living life, I have to take the consequences. I cannot be free from them. When I resist God's will for me in Christ, I am resisting my own true self, the life God intended me to live. I cannot escape from the ultimate realities of my situation. They are backed up by the Almighty. I can only break myself against the universe when I persist in following ungodly dreams and believing in things that never can be so. I believe in the Almighty.

... almighty

Why does the Almighty need *me* if *he* has always had all power? Why do I have to keep working and praying for his cause if he is already almighty without me? Only because he has chosen to work out a world where the help of people like me is necessary! God could create a new heaven and a new earth right now by a single word. But that world would have to be a simple world of machines and robots that engineers could easily make. Only God has the resources and patience necessary for making the kind of world he has undertaken to set up. God is working toward a world of free people who really want to live together, loving

35

God and men, despite the fact that those same people could just as easily turn the whole thing into a hell. The Almighty has taken on a truly God-sized job— but is any lesser goal so worthy? To accomplish his deliberately chosen purpose, God must have our co-operation. Our willing help is an essential part of his plan. Since he has chosen to have us for fellow work-men, the Almighty needs us as such. He will have his project completed eventually, even if I and many others don't go along with him. We may be able to prolong his working time, but we can no more block his way forever than men can permanently and com-pletely dam back a mountain torrent. He can overrule even our worst deeds so that eventually they will issue in unexpectedly good results. At the game of life, God will always have the last move. When all of us have played our last, it will only take one more move by the Almighty to win the game. He wields the powers of creation and resurrection—the powers of ultimate vic-tory.

Is God still the Almighty outside the fortress of heaven? Would he shine as the victor if he had to struggle for life as we do? God loves the world and came into it to rescue us. He had to live under our conditions in order to rescue us, facing every kind of threat this world can muster. In Jesus he was born among strangers in a stable. As a helpless baby he depended on human arms just as I did. As a child his life was threatened by a vicious king. He went through the whole process of growing up. He suffered among us what we suffer, and he never spared himself, not even from a cruel death. We mighty men stretched him out and nailed him to the beams of a wooden cross. But we couldn't kill his love for us. We even sealed his corpse away underground behind a great stone. Some God he seemed! The weakest of the weak! But even in his weakness the Almighty was stronger than our strongest acts. He rolled away our big stone and sat on it! There he was, alive again, still offering us his life-giving love. We simply couldn't drive him away! "Lo, I am with you always." The Almighty is willing to become our Suffering Servant. He even asks our permission to give us his love and life in place of our sin and death. He wins our hearts, not by the raw force of tyrannical compulsion, but by the overpowering winsomeness of his love. No one has stooped lower than the Almighty, but he will conquer.

. . . almighty, maker . . .

As soon as I tell the world that I believe in one almighty Creator God who loves like a Father, I have to face a blast of hostile voices. "If there is a God like that, why did he make such a dreadful world?" Everybody knows that living in this world is by no means one long, uninterrupted, idyllic, luxurious, lovely and delightful experience. There is poverty, strife, treachery, disease, disaster, and death. The most faithful soul must cry, "Why, O why?" Even Jesus had his dark hours. So what shall I say? Jesus never explained these great problems. But he did do something about them. He fed the hungry. His spirit of humble, forgiving, serving love brought peace, reconciliation, and brotherhood. His loyalty to truth, at whatever cost, opened a spring of honesty that flowed far and wide into the world. He healed the sick and offered men an eternal life that would see them through any disaster and death. The kind of life that Jesus poured into the world has done great things in relieving and preventing distress. But nevertheless Jesus himself came to a cross. Surely, if there is any way around human suffering, God would have found it for such a wonderful person as his own Son. But Jesus was spared nothing. There must be sufficient reasons for the existence of evil in the world, even though we don't yet know what they are. Someday I shall understand. But whether I understand or not, I still have to live in the same troublous world. It certainly won't help me to face this world more adequately if I turn my back on the Savior who has done so much to remove the problems I have to face.

I think I can understand some of the reasons why what I call evil has to exist in this created world. (After all, this is a *created* world. It is not God.) For example, this world from the beginning contained something of the nothingness out of which it was created. There had to be a kind of nothingness called space in between things to separate them and give them room to move and change and live, choosing directions. But when things move into empty spaces, smashups and blowups are possible, to say nothing of wrong choices, strife, and death. A created world is bound to be dangerous. Is it better to create a world in which the possibilities are both wonderful and terrible, or not to create any world at all? God decided that it was worth risking tragedies like the cross if a person like Jesus could appear in the world he would create. God gave men enough intelligence to control or avoid the world's dangerous threats. But we misuse our brains, our freedom, and God's world. God did something even about our misdoing by giving us Jesus Christ, whom we promptly reject. God has given us everything we need to make the most of this world. We ourselves are the real problem of evil. It's up to us to stop our nonsense and get on with God's work instead of complaining about the way he made the world. No man has ever thought up a kind of world which hadn't the slightest possibility of evil in it, and which any human being would want to live in. I still trust in the Almighty Creator in whom Jesus trusted.

. . . maker of heaven and earth

Suddenly the solemn statement, "I believe in the maker of heaven and earth," sounds a little tinny and bumptious. In fact it's almost ridiculous. Here I am, a mere speck of dust lost in the immensity of the stars, and space, and time, piping up with my little opinion about the One who made it all. More important than my belief in the Creator is the fact that the Creator believed in *me*. He not only made heaven and earth, but he must also have considered that it was a good thing to make me. Otherwise I wouldn't be here either to believe or disbelieve in him. God cares so much about me that he has given me my life and his world and his Son.

He has provided for me in so many wonderful ways that I could easily fool myself into thinking that I myself must be the center of the universe. If he went to all that trouble for me, he really must believe in me. So I am not merely a speck of dust or an illusion. But I must always remember that I am not God. He alone is the Creator, while I am only a creature among fellow creatures. I depend on the Almighty for my existence and powers. If God were to doze off for a moment, that would be the end of me. When my day is done, God will still go on. I'm so very changeable, but God is consistent. Death is a threat to me, but death has no dominion over him. It is clear that I am not God. I must suspect the appeal of any religion that would help me to worship myself or make me out to be so much a god that I might try either to defy the living God, or to take over his powers and rule in his place, even overrule God.

It is also clear to me that none of my fellow creatures is God. None of them has the right to take God's place in my life. Nature is not God. Once upon a time everything I now see around me did not exist; it had to be made. I must never worship nature or anything else in this world, however beautiful and poetical such worship may seem. I must never get so fascinated with this world that I forget that my first responsibility is to the God who made the world for his purposes, not mine. The world belongs to the God who created it. Nothing in it is ever really mine. Nor is anything in it outside the reach of God.

The *whole* world belongs to its Maker, not just a religious part that some people call sacred or spiritual. Every place belongs to God, not just special places for worship. Every house, every land, every place of work or play, belongs to the Creator. All time belongs to God, not just special times for prayer and worship. Every hour, by day or by night throughout all the years of history, belongs to the Creator by right. There is no corner of any man's life that is exempt from God's claims. If he puts things into our hands to hold and use in trust for him, we are responsible to him for everything we do. Nothing is mine, all mine. I cannot protest if he asks me to give him back what he loaned to me. He can do what he wants to do with his own. "The Lord gave, and the Lord has taken away; blessed be the name of the Lord."

41

. . . *maker of heaven and earth*

I can't imagine what it would be like to be God the Creator. Someone should invent a new word to describe God's unique kind of existence. There just isn't anything known on this earth that is more than merely *somewhat like* the Maker of all. I'm nervous about trying to prove that God *exists* if God's "existence" is so unlike any kind of existence which we know. Human language and thought are utterly unable to arrive at an understanding of God. As for me, I'm content to let God speak for himself in his own terms, as he did in Jesus Christ. I know that *Jesus* existed. I know he had power over nature and life and death. All I need to know about God is that he is like Jesus. This simple knowledge saves me from making up a religion of wild guesses, and gods in the image of myself.

I don't know how God "exists," nor do I know how he made all things that exist. When *I* make something, I only reshape some existing material or rearrange something I already have. I may make paint from colored substances, canvas from cotton, and a painting from both, but I can never *create* anything. God is the only one who can create without preexisting material. Creation is an activity peculiar to God alone! It is unique; I don't know how he does it. God is still at work creating the universe in the process which we call time, steadily transforming his world, making all things new to the farthest reaches of space. Every moment of history is different from every other moment. If everything that happens has the hand of the Creator in it, then I cannot understand fully any event whatsoever, because I can't understand how God creates it. If I forget this, I might easily think that mankind can learn everything there is to be known. But when I recognize the presence of the Creator in any situation, a due and proper humility comes over me. Then I approach the natural world with a wholesome sense of awe and respect. The simplest thing is too deep for the greatest minds. There's a mystery about existence that brings me to worship, for everything that exists is a wonder from the creating hand of God. But worship does not excuse me from painstaking scientific investigation by which I shall try to know *exactly* what God has done in making his world. Worship and science should go hand in hand throughout God's creation.

When I was a youngster I used to ask "Who made God?" Now I see that this is as meaningless a question as "How heavy is green?" Greenness has nothing to do with heaviness, and likewise God is not a makeable creature. Just as I have to accept the fact that light travels at a fixed speed, so I have to accept a Maker who was not made.

... *maker of heaven and earth*

Why did God create the world? From all eternity, the loving communion of Father-Son-Holy Ghost was fully and completely self-sufficient. God was not driven to create the world by some inner need. He was not starving, or poor, or lonely. Nor did he make the world one day just because of a chance whim or a passing fancy. It was simply that the perfect love between Father-Son-Holy Ghost was so glorious that there ought to be more like it. Something so infinitely valuable ought to be infinitely multiplied.

So God set out to build a world like a palace of mirrors which would reflect the light of the Trinity's holy love from every possible direction. He would make only things that could do this. Thus, to banish darkness, emptiness, and formlessness, God said, "Let there be light!" And there was light. Then he made his created light into matter. There arose before him an unbelievable multitude of ingenious substances with a host of incredible functions. He brought some of this dead stuff to life and made all kinds of living things. In his workshop—this world—God has continually been making new things out of old, working up his first basic materials into ever higher and higher forms. The lower gave up its existence for the higher —a sort of elementary sacrifice that foreshadowed

Christ's fulfilling sacrifice. Every one of them tends to hold together in unity and wholeness for its lifetime. Thus each atom and cell, each organism and planet, reflects in its own way something of the unity and wholeness of Father-Son-Holy Ghost. Stones always seem so silent to me, but Jesus said that to the ear of God they ceaselessly cry out their praise of his holy love. Throughout millions of years God has enjoyed his work and his creatures.

When God was about to make man, he paused before opening this tremendous new chapter of his creation. Into man's being and powers he would put all the processes which he had already worked out in the lower realms of creation—and a great deal more. As the ground is for plants, and as plants are for animals, and all of them for man, so man would be specially for God. In being gathered up into man, all lesser things would share in the glory of man. And it would be man's glory to bear the image of God, to be consciously and willingly the reflector of God's holy love. God's Son was so in love with the whole project that he was prepared to die to bring it to pass. He would join himself to the earth, to live out in it the greatest love possible to a creature. Even if all other men failed to fulfill their destiny, the Son of God as Son of man would bring all creatures and all history to their highest meaning and fulfillment in himself. In Jesus Christ the whole world which God had made, man and all, was gathered up to show forth the perfection of God's holy love. Christ was found worthy to inherit the world's power and riches, wisdom and strength, honor, glory, and blessing. His song of love was sung to God on behalf of all creation. In him God had achieved his great goal at least once in history. In Christ we have the key to the purpose of God's whole creation, especially to the meaning of man.

... *maker of heaven and earth*

If God made the world, then it must be basically good. The world didn't happen by accident. It's far too ingeniously contrived and organized and understandable for me to believe that. God fully intended to make this world, and he loves it. He committed himself to a purpose which required this kind of world, including flesh and blood, sex and work. These and all the rest of it fit into his plan. There is nothing that he made that he despises. Nothing that he made is too low for him or irrelevant. God has bound himself seriously and unreservedly to the world he has made. Every moment he confirms his original decision to create this world by upholding his world and preserving its existence.

He dramatically reconfirmed his interest in this world by entering it through Jesus Christ, when he became flesh and dwelt among us. Jesus was a real part of this world. He enjoyed eating. He got tired. He

sneezed in dust. His hands got dirty like hands everywhere. Jesus was at least part of nature, flesh, history,
the world. He concerned himself with the worldly well-
being of individuals, families, his nation, and mankind.
On the cross he participated in the pain and suffering
sacrifices of all creatures. When Christ rose from the
dead, his *body* rose with him to an entirely new level
of being. The world of matter, flesh, and nature that
God made has certainly not gone untouched by Christ's
work. He is supremely relevant to the vast enterprise
of the material world where human life is set. Christ
came to carry all lower forms of this world up with
him to new heights. That's what his ascension means.
God was in Christ reconciling the world, the whole
created world, to himself. It was to this world that he
returned in his Holy Spirit.

In view of God's obvious love for the world I must
give the world its full value, and I must respect the
whole world. There is a right and proper worldliness
which I must share with God. I must take my full
place in this world if ever I am to be entrusted with
another place in a world to come.

God made this wonderful world, and I am part of it
all. What a privilege to be alive, to look upon it with
amazement and gratitude, and to feel its glory in my
bones! I am only the dust of the earth, yet I can rise
up at the call of God. When I rise up, the world that
fed me, the race that gave me birth, also rise up. When
I worship, all plants and animals which died that I
might keep on living participate in my praise. In Christ

something of the earth ascended into the very presence of God. This is the promise of things to come, that what Christ gathers up from this earth will be part of a new heaven and a new earth. There, everything will shine ever so clearly with the glory of the Creator God whose name is Love. I must carry my world with me into Christ and so into the eternal glory.

and in Jesus Christ . . .

The Creed is a continued story. I have said, "I believe in God the Father Almighty, maker of heaven and earth." Before you can say "So what?" I must go right on to tell of what God did with his world, what he is doing with it, and what he will do with it through Jesus Christ, his Son. The Creator is by no means like a fitful hobbyist who once tried his hand at world-making but quickly gave it up, abandoning the incomplete project forever. I believe that God's first creating was only a beginning. There is an "and" to it, which leads on directly to the story of Jesus Christ. The Almighty could not be called "Father" Almighty without a Son. Mere belief in a God who made heaven and earth is not enough for me. I need to have some notion of what he made it for. What does God expect of me, one of his creatures? Without Jesus Christ I frankly don't have a likely clue. And neither has anyone else.

Without Jesus, everything dangles like the dot under a cosmic question mark. My slightest move in Christ's direction is a move toward the ultimate answer to my ultimate questions. For fuller understanding of myself, the world, and our destiny in the Creator Father, I must know more and more about Jesus, his only Son, our Lord.

Who, then, was Jesus? This is the most important question that anyone can ever ask. Whatever answer I give in my heart largely decides what road I shall travel through life and what the end of my journey will be. Jesus Christ is the Way, the Truth, and the Life.

Jesus was real. He was at least a human being much like me in many ways. He was no make-believe, storybook hero dreamed up by some teller of tales in the land of the Jews. When he was born into the family of Mary and Joseph, he was a flesh and blood baby who had to be looked after just the same as the other children who came along later. His brothers and sisters saw him washing up for lunch, getting his hair cut, and trying on new sandals. While the little ones played with shavings in Joseph's carpenter shop, Jesus was learning his trade. They all knew that slivers, cuts, and blisters hurt his hands the same as theirs. After a long day's work Jesus was tired and hungry. This big brother of their's spoke and dressed like everybody else.

But as Jesus gained experience of the life around his home and the village of Nazareth with its synagogue, its visitors, its fields, and hills, he gradually came to seem

somehow different from the neighbor boys. He never
lost his childlike trust in God, while the other young
men became worldly wise. He never lost his simple,
straightforward honesty, while the others learned how to
conceal their meanness under a polish of politeness,
with a show of respectability and religion. Jesus was
never self-consciously concerned about developing his
own reputation for righteousness. He just loved people
and wanted God's best for them. In the process he
showed himself to be good, clear through. Jesus discovered how to be good without trying.

and in Jesus Christ . . .

When a little child looks steadily into my eyes, I
feel mighty uncomfortable, even guilty. In a way Jesus
was like an unspoiled child or a newly arrived visitor
from a clean, faraway world. He saw our human ways
clearly for what they are and made men take a new
look at themselves. In his presence many people felt
uncomfortable at first, especially those whose high position in society depended on nobody finding out what
they were really like. For Jesus reality counted, not
mere appearances. He was an embarrassment to men
who went through the impressive motions of religion
when all the time they were really worshiping power,
prestige, and wealth—not God. He could always detect

the social climbers, elbowing and scheming their way to places of honor. He saw how respected men *seemed* to keep to the letter of God's law but actually went dead against the spirit of it, justifying themselves by all sorts of ridiculous excuses and fine hairsplitting. There was too much pious talk going on in religious circles and not enough genuine service of God. Praising ideals is one thing; actually living up to them is another. There was too much imitation of righteousness, show-off charity without love, pride in humility, and a studied holiness reserved for appropriate occasions. Too many people thought they could buy the grace of God in the Temple, as they could buy favors from the guests they entertained. The consistency, simplicity, and directness of Jesus' life really upset all men of deceit.

If falsity bothered Jesus, lovelessness bothered him even more. People were so heartlessly self-centered, without concern for the rest of humanity. But in Jesus' eyes the human needs of others took precedence even over important religious rules of personal righteousness. The venerable observation of the sabbath came second to feeding the hungry or restoring the crippled. For him, people always had priority over principles. One man restored to sanity was worth far more to him than a whole herd of pigs. Jesus saw not social classes but persons; not crowds but individuals. He noticed people and had time for them, even though they were called nobodies and sinners. Jesus was the friend of the outcasts and the downtrodden in the social system of his day. He was convinced that loveless men and their systems are doomed.

Jesus saw through people's pitiful pretences. But when they realized that he still loved them, a breath of the fresh air of honesty often swept over them. Jesus accepted them, even though he did not entirely approve of their lives at the moment. They could be themselves in the presence of his understanding love, and they could make a new start in life. The loving truth of Jesus was a real tonic. His presence was the power of new life. So Jesus came to know that he could develop men into what their Creator had always intended them to be. He therefore proclaimed the good news, the gospel, that in himself God's power had come to deliver men. But big men who lived by lies and deceit, who shamelessly exploited the poor and weak, saw that this man of truth and love was a dangerous threat to their whole setup. Hence the Cross.

and in Jesus Christ . . .

"Call his name Jesus, for he will save his people from their sins." That's what the voice of heaven told Mary and Joseph. "Jesus" was a common enough name in those times. But giving this name to this particular child was loaded with faith. "Jesus" meant "God is Savior." Christians have called Jesus Light, Shepherd, Master, Lord, Priest, Lamb, Mediator, Redeemer,

Water, Bread, Resurrection, Life, and many other names. Each of these titles is really a way of saying that Jesus is the Savior of men. Whatever else I may call him, Jesus is what God called him—Savior! This name describes what he came to be and to do: to seek and to save that which was lost. The name that Mary murmured over his manger was later written over his cross. Although the name was given to him, its meaning was for others. He saved others; himself he could not save. His destiny was to be the Savior of others. The name "Jesus" relates him to us. We need a Savior. We get out of control, guilty, enslaved. We feel alone, meaningless, lost, trapped, helplessly perishing. We are unloved, unloving, frustrated, fed up. We are entangled in a network of lies, overpowering systems, and conflicting claims that tug us in a dozen different directions. But we have a Savior! Jesus is a name of hope, a name of promise, a name of power. By Jesus the Savior I have been saved, I am being saved, and I will be saved ultimately and forever. He saves me *from* every state of sin and misery sooner or later, and he saves me *for* God. He saves me from human enemies and the judgment of God, for the sonship and blessing of God, for likeness to God in service to his world.

The name of Jesus glorified everything he touched and gave it a higher value. We must call his land the "holy land." His people are the holy church. God grant the coming of the day when the name of Jesus the Savior may be truthfully written upon all homes, all factories, offices, stores, mills, and classrooms. Most of us want the name of Jesus the Savior called over us at our baptisms, our weddings, and our funerals. May it be meaningful over us on every ordinary day, everywhere and always. We need a Savior, a personal power, a powerful person, to come to us from beyond to set things right with us. The perversity of the world has always beaten every mere reformer who tried to change it. Men's moral efforts, efficient organizations, scientific achievements, and cultural education are not enough. We still need a Savior. Without God for us, with us, and in us, we're beaten. Jesus the Savior has had a deeper and more wholesome effect on the quality of human life around the world than any other man or group of men. I believe that the future belongs to Jesus!

and in Jesus Christ . . .

Jesus is the Christ of God, the hope of Israel and all the earth. The Jews had dreamed that God would send them a leader who would bring them into a golden age of security, prosperity, and justice, with power over all nations. This great leader, like their other kings, priests, and prophets, would be set apart for his work by the pouring of God's holy oil upon his head. The "anointed leader," the "one poured upon," was called in Hebrew "'the Messiah" and in Greek "the Christ." To call Jesus the Christ is to claim that he fulfilled God's promises of a Messiah for Israel, promises which are recorded in the Old Testament. I believe that Jesus was foreshadowed by the biblical prophets, priests, and kings, but that he was very much more than any or all of them. He set those ancient themes in a higher key. Jesus spent much of his teaching time trying to lift the eyes of his followers beyond the horizon of their own nation, its material prosperity, and political power. He was more the Christ of God's dreams than the Messiah of Jewish hopes. The Jewish notion of Christ was far too small for the scope of God's plans. Jesus *had* been sent by God and empowered by the Spirit of God. He *would* deliver all people who would receive him as their Savior. He *was* establishing a kingdom, one that would spread throughout the world. He *would* bring real peace, security, and justice by changing men's inner lives, but not by using external force. His new order would offer far greater blessings than the old arrangement with Israel. Jesus resolved to win men's hearts by suffering for them and serving them, not by military conquest. God gave him his entire approval as his Christ and raised him from the dead with all power on earth and in heaven. Right now, in God's own realm, Jesus is Christ, the King. He is the kingdom-center of those who acknowledge him, the judge of all men. His will overrules even those who reject him.

When I call Jesus "Christ," I declare that he is no ordinary man. I believe that he is God's special agent to bring to pass God's plans for his world. I believe that Jesus knows the secret counsels of God, that he is closer to the mind of the Almighty than anyone else has ever been. If Jesus is Christ, his claim upon me is God's own claim, the highest claim of all, second to no other. If I utterly disown him, I disqualify myself from my God-given destiny in this world and consign myself to the cosmic garbage dump, a self-made exile from the kingdom of God. If Jesus is the Christ of God, he is the Christ for God's whole world. Notice that "Christ" is the Greek word for a Hebrew idea. All that God had offered to the Hebrews, and more, God now offers also to the Greeks and to all men. The Christ commands, "Go into all the world and preach the gospel to the whole creation."

. . . *his only Son* . . .

How do I single Jesus Christ out of all mankind as God's appointed Savior? Nearly everyone does saving work of some kind, meeting somebody's serious needs. I couldn't have got along without all my helpers, my saviors, such as the armed forces, policemen, garbage collectors, teachers, repairmen, doctors, ministers, farmers, and parents. Many a statesmen and hero has been remembered as "the savior of his people." Which of all these do I mean when I speak of my Savior? To specify exactly the one I'm talking about, I add to the name of Jesus Christ the words, "his only Son our Lord." Then I give a little sketch of his life, as the Creed does. That will set Jesus apart from all other saviors.

I hail Jesus as God's appointed Savior and God's only Son because God himself set Jesus apart from all other men. He was the only one out of mankind's millions of dead that God ever brought back for all time. This fact by itself doesn't prove much of anything. But considering that Jesus made himself out to be the Son of God, it would be most unlikely for the God of truth to bring him back if he hadn't been the one he claimed he was. While Jesus didn't make a practice of going around telling everybody point-blank that he was the Son of God, he did just about everything else imaginable to leave exactly that impression on his friends. Even his enemies among the Jews got his message quite clearly and therefore had him put to death for blasphemy. I can't explain the cross without Jesus' claim to be the Son of God. He certainly talked as though he were on the most intimate terms with his "Father in heaven" and as though he had real inside knowledge of "the Son." He forgave sins, and who but God has the right to do that? He dared extend God's law much deeper and further than when God had given it to Moses. By the sheer power of his word, just as if he were the Creator, Jesus took control of the winds and waves and nature. If he did these things only by trickery, they would be hard to reconcile with his courageous truthfulness and concern for people. Surely God would not choose to honor such a bold-faced liar by bringing him back to life and by exalting his power and existence so far beyond other men's! What God did puts aside all past and future opinions about who Jesus was. The Almighty backed up everything that Jesus had assumed and claimed for himself. Occasionally a man may wonder whether a certain child is really his own child. But the Lord God didn't make a mistake when he pointed out Jesus to the world as his only Son. No one else has ever stood that way in the divine spotlight. Because God thus openly recognized his Son, thoughtful men, taking account of all the facts, also acknowledge that Jesus is the only Son of God.

. . . his only Son, our Lord

Jesus Christ is God's eternal Son. His sonship was not a sometime thing. I believe that he came from God as life springs from life. Although he was always the same kind as God, he added to himself the created nature of humankind as well. From all eternity the Son was involved in the very being of the Father. I believe that God always thinks of himself and his ways with the world in terms of his Son. When God looks in the mirror, he sees Jesus. When God created the universe, he had in mind specific purposes enwrapped in his Son and saw in him a shining vision of what the world's future, with him in it, could be. If the Spirit of the Son could dwell in men, they too could be called sons of God and he could take them into his family. I believe that, in Jesus Christ, God has given us the way to become no less than sons of God, with a share in God's eternal future.

Jesus Christ is far more than most men give him credit for. I never feel right when someone calls him "a great teacher." He certainly *was* that. But a teacher who leads people to believe that he is the Son of God come to save the world, when he is only a mere man, shouldn't be allowed to teach anybody. Nor do I see how anyone can even call Jesus "the best man who ever lived" if he deceived people into thinking he was the Son of God when he really wasn't. It bothers me too when ardent disciples of some "ism" or society claim that Jesus was the first or finest example of their political principles, their economic schemes or ways of doing things. Jesus is away beyond the top of any human heap. If God has recognized Jesus as his beloved Son and placed him over every earthly power, can men recognize him as being less?

Those who believe that Jesus wields God's authority over them are held together by him as the hub of a wheel holds all its spokes together. The Son of God thus brings into being a cluster of Christians, a community of believers which we call the church. The Son of God is this church's possessor, owner, master, director, judge and center; in short, its Lord. Christians are all his. We are in his power and for him. When I say that I believe in Jesus Christ, *our Lord,* I am speaking as one of this fellowship of the faithful, as one of the many members of his church. Christ's lordship over his church sets him apart from all other "saviors," and at the same time sets churchmen apart from all other men. Our Lord is identified by the Christian stream that runs through history. From time to time some powerful dictator or party claims the total loyalty and obedience of men without respect to right and wrong. But for Christians, Christ's commands outrank all others. He alone has the right to claim them totally. If some ruler's wishes conflict with the Spirit of Jesus Christ, Christians ought not to disobey Jesus. They have often died at the hands of frustrated authorities, rather than be false to their Lord.

... *our Lord*

If Jesus Christ is my Lord, every day I shall have to choose between Christ's claim upon me and all pulls and pressures which would take me away from him. As a Christian, I have to sit loosely to "the gang" and "the system." The important question is not what others want me to do and be. My life's direction must be determined by the *Lord,* not by my ambitions and interests or by the possibility of more fame, fun, or finances.

The church of the Creed is daily marked by its choosing between "our Lord" and all the would-be lords who woo its favor.

I must always be careful how I use the world "our" with respect to the Lord. It shouldn't sound self-righteous and nasty, as when some snip of a child says, *"Our* family is better than *your* family because *we* own a racing yacht!" The "our" in "our Lord" is intended to say much more about the Lord than it says about us. Nobody owns him! "Our" shouldn't sound boastful and patronizing like "That's our boy!" Nor do I want to sound like a dog in the manger, implying, "Jesus is our own private Lord, for us alone; and all you others, keep your hands off!" The Christian fellowship must always keep itself open so that the outsider can become an insider when he comes to acknowledge the same Lord. Indeed, Christ has commanded us to go out seeking to bring the others in, if they will come.

Christ is Lord of all. He is the Lord of the others whether they want to recognize him as such or not. Sooner or later, in one way or another, they will have to meet their Lord and bow their knee. Our Lord is Lord of far more than his church. He has the whole world in his hands, ruling and overruling all things. All the crowns belong on his head. So the "our" in "our Lord" not only implies the oneness of all Christians, but also the oneness of the Christians with the whole human race and the whole created world.

If Jesus is the acknowledged Lord of the church, his word is bond and rule for the church. If any group of people is to get along together, they must agree to obey some principle of authority, some law or Lord. Imagine two teams trying to play some game without rules or referee! What Jesus said and did has become his rule for his church. The Bible contains the record of what Jesus said and did, and how the earliest Christians understood all this. Thus the Bible has an authority in the church which is derived from our Lord's authority. And the Holy Ghost, the Spirit of our Lord, is with us, to help us interpret the Bible and guide our behavior. We therefore consider the Old Testament, for example, in the light of the Spirit of Jesus Christ. He is the Lord of the Bible, as well as the Lord of Christians and the church. We judge our doings in the light of the word and Spirit of Jesus Christ. The church is not our lord, nor are we churchmen entitled to lord it over others, forcing them to conform to our notions against their will. Christ is the Lord, not we.

who was conceived by the Holy Ghost

The life story of our Lord has its roots away back, before there were any beginnings. He was himself the beginning of the world's story, and he will be its end. Yet he did make a new beginning on this earth as human flesh and blood in the land of the Jews. There that baby was born who cleft history into two; into B.C. and

A.D. Even the big bomb didn't do that! The world has never been the same since the Son of God was enfleshed here. His "en-man-ment" established history's center and ultimate meaning. Because he came we know how precious we are in God's sight, and what tremendous possibilities he has opened up for us. Because the Lord stood on the same ground with us, this world will always shine with a kind of glory that nothing can altogether becloud.

Why did he come? He loved us more than he loved all the power he possessed in heaven, more than he loved unstained garments of light. The Son of God laid aside all his splendor to become one of our human race, whose very name had smelled to high heaven! I just don't get it. It's utterly beyond my wits to explain why he would come to this stable of beasts. Like a little child I'll have to say, "It was just because. . . ." Because God loves us. Because that's the way God is. Oh, who can *reason* his way into the secret heart of divine love?

And who can understand how the unfenced God could wear the skin of a little child? Would the One who bestraddles the abyss of space get hurt if his mother dropped him on the floor? Though thunderbolts leave the Almighty unscathed, men would pierce him with nails. The great Giver of life was destined to die. The timeless One began to have birthdays. The beginning of all things was born. They couldn't tell the Creator of the universe from a creature born in a barn. Such statements sound completely whacky to some of my brainy friends who claim to know what

God can do and can't do. The "God" they have
dreamed up wouldn't even think of such things, let
alone try to do them! But then I can't expect their
man-made "God" to be capable of doing any of the
things that the true God is always doing. Who could
have predicted that God would make exactly this kind
of world and none other? Light didn't have to travel
just so fast and no faster. The Almighty could have
made hosts of creatures quite different from those he
actually chose to make. God writes his own prescrip-
tions and draws his own blueprints without consulting
us as to what he may do or may not do. He is God.
If he chose to enter this world's history through the
small door of a woman's body, that's his business. It's
only one more surprise in a world full of surprises. He
can step down his voltage to keep from scorching us,
and step into our midst if he wants to. This was God's
doing. Jesus Christ was conceived by the Holy Spirit
of *God*.

. . . *conceived by the Holy Ghost*

Men are deep-dyed "do-it-yourselfers." The other
religions, as well as the heresies of Christianity, show us
how we can save ourselves and be our own god. We
want to be proud of what we have done by ourselves.
As "self-made men who worship their creator," we re-

sent being told that God has had to help us. But any religion which denies that God became man in Jesus cuts vital power lines. For by joining our human nature to his own, the Son of God prepared the way for us men to be received in peace and joy by God forever. Jesus made available to us on our level, by his Spirit, the power to live lives like his, victorious and eternal. It was a new creation, for he breathed into mankind the breath of his own wonderful life.

It was God who planned this and God's power that brought it to pass. God in his mercy took the initiative and came to our rescue. It is not that we men sought for God and finally found him, but that God came to seek us out. God has never been lost, but we have! Without him we can do nothing much. As a woman without a man is powerless to bear a child, so the human race was powerless to produce its own savior. Neither Jesus' relatives, the Jewish people, the Holy Land, nor the Roman Empire, are enough to explain the presence of a Jesus among them. He was by no means a natural product of his times, inevitably thrown up by the processes of humanity and history. Jesus was sent. He didn't just happen. He was the earthly embodiment of the eternal Son of God. He was conceived by the Holy Ghost before he was born of the Virgin Mary. Our Lord's entrance into this world was effected by the same Creator Spirit who had moved upon the face of the deep when the earth was a-borning. Once again the Holy Spirit hovered over the turbulent waters of humanity and enabled a Jewish girl to bring forth Jesus. No man planned it, willed it, or had a part in it. He was conceived by the Holy Ghost.

Being a Christian today means having the Spirit of the Lord within me. I know right well I didn't put him there. He even made me willing to open the door! The word of Christ was always coming to me through my family, my friends, and my church. But it took root in me by the Holy Spirit, and by the Holy Spirit it grew into Christ-life within me. Many years passed before I realized that he had been working within. But my parents were right to have me baptized as a child, for he really was working even then. He isn't through yet. Who can say when I first began to be Christian? The Holy Spirit works quietly when and where he wills, even in the babies of Christian homes. Mary did not understand what was happening in her, and neither do Christians-in-the-making. Every Christian is a work of the Holy Spirit.

born of the Virgin Mary

Both the Bible and the Creed lay emphasis on the agency of God and the fact that Jesus was actually born, more than on Mary's virginity. At this late date, or even in earliest Christian times, no one could prove anything about the virginity of Jesus' mother. It has always been a matter of faith. After all, the paternity of any child is likewise largely a matter of faith in his

mother's story. I believe . . . in Jesus . . . born of
the Virgin Mary. Biological scientists no longer say
that a virgin birth is impossible. Nor should theolo-
gians say that Jesus absolutely had to be born of a
virgin. Only God knows about Jesus. The Scriptures
don't use the virgin birth of Jesus to prove any essential
doctrine. They simply record it and pass on to other
matters. So do I.

Mary's part in our Lord's story must not be under-
played. As a male, I note that God chose a woman for
the honor of bringing his Son into the world. Christian men must realize that God does not share their
prejudices concerning women. Mary was amazed that
God knew that a little nobody like her even existed.
But God has his eye on all of us, even the lowliest.
Even I can be swept into the current of God's great
plan. Although Mary couldn't explain things to her-
self or to anyone else, she still murmured her faithful
obedience to God. I must not wait until God answers
all my questions before I begin obeying him. Mary
had "found favor with God," but nevertheless she came
into great trouble over her son. God's favor doesn't
promise me a lifetime of unbroken happiness. Mary
could not prove that the child she bore was the Son
of God. Only God could vindicate her, and he did. As
I take up my deeply personal task of bearing Christ to
the world, risking my reputation among the worldly
wise, only God can vindicate me by honoring my work
with fruitfulness. Mary has a glory all her own as well
as the common glory of Christian faith. All generations,

including mine, must call her blessed, but we need not deck her with false jewels. Mary needed a Savior too. Through her, God came down low enough, once and for all, to hear our prayers even today. We need not use Mary as our errand girl.

Jesus was born. The Son of God really became part of the human race. He bridged the great gulf between the Creator and his creatures, between the Holy God and sinful men. What is God's can now come to man, and man can come freely to God. God used Mary, an earthly means, to accomplish his purpose. He used the intricate arrangements of birth to bring his Son into the world. Since Jesus came, a new glory has surrounded childbearing, motherhood, and home.

Christmas in my home must never be greedy, gaudy, or guzzling. The birth of Jesus contains such profound meanings that silent wonder, breaking forth into joyous praise, is the proper response. May God help me and my family to redeem Christmas. We can at least make it a birthday celebration for Jesus and invite him to come. I hope that our Guest will not be forgotten. And I hope that we will not forget that we are really *his* guests at God's great feast!

suffered . . .

Surprise after surprise in this Creed! God created a world out of nothing and was born into it. Then, of all things, he suffered in his own world! If God is all good, why did he allow suffering in his world? If God is all mighty, why did he himself undergo suffering? How about that?

Suffering is more than pain. Although I certainly don't like pain, I'm glad that God built this alarm system into me to warn me when I'm in danger. The doctors and I can usually do something about pain and its causes. But they don't have any pills or shots to help me when I clench my hands and groan in agony: "Why, oh why, did all this have to happen? Why did I do it? If I had only thought! What will become of me now?" Such questions and probings about human destiny, about the wellsprings of meaning, and about far-reaching personal relationships arise far beyond pain, in deep suffering. I suffer when disasters happen to things and people who are precious to me. I suffer when I share someone else's trouble.

Why couldn't God have made a world without any suffering in it? God could easily have made a lot of unsuffering stones, all looking alike and not minding which stone was where. As long as they only sat there, without weathering or collisions, all would be well, I suppose. But they would merely exist. They wouldn't care about what happened to other stones. They couldn't decide either to be what they were, or not to be what they were. This would be a "perfect" world— perfect without suffering, and perfectly dead! We men are good at manufacturing unsuffering identical machines on assembly lines. But God has taken on the

God-sized project of putting together a world made of people. He has created unique individuals, sensitive and alive, alert and a-loving, with freedom to change and decide their ways. People are so much more than machines.

A world of people necessarily contains the possibilities for either distressful suffering, or for loving peace. Men can easily turn God's world into a torture chamber. But it could also become a world where people really want to live together, reflecting in all their relationships the glory of the interpersonal love of God, the Holy Trinity. To make us human, God had to make us free. It's not his fault that we've usually chosen to distort his world into what is almost the opposite of his hoped-for kingdom of peace. But suffering or no suffering, I'd rather be a man than a stone or a machine. It's better to have lived and loved and suffered as a human being than never to have lived at all.

suffered . . .

I can't think of any other way to make a human sort of world than the way God made it. The only "perfect world" that I can dream up inevitably turns out to be either the solitary splendor of God, or a lifeless realm of the dead. But whenever I have acted in "solitary splendor" as though I were the lordly center of the universe, I have created a wasteland of suffering around me. Somebody will surely suffer if I try to live as though I were *really* in a make-believe world of my own—a world God never made—doing things that God has clearly forbidden. Unbelief in the goodness and wisdom of God will always lead me to bitterness in my times of trial.

Jesus Christ our Lord suffered! Our Lord became thoroughly a man, exposed to suffering. The Son of God as the Son of man walked with us through the burning fiery furnace. He drank up the cup of human suffering right to the very last drop. Mary and Joseph knew all about anxiety and poverty on the night Jesus was born. Soon they became refugees in Egypt. Jesus was always like a stranger in his own family and hometown. Nobody understood him. The ideals and practices of his people outraged his deep sense of the importance of reality and compassion. Years passed by as he wrestled in spirit and in prayer with what to do about it. Though he felt intensely about the unnecessary suffering men were causing, he had to wait and wait. Sometimes he was strongly tempted to take up the ways of the world's troublers, to beat them at their own game. But he firmly resolved to be faithful to the principle that only truth and love will really change the world and eliminate unnecessary suffering.

Jesus knew that the forces that fatten on falsity would mount an attack on his truth. He knew that the greedy, proud ones would find his concern for all people a

71

menace. For Jesus, the way to end suffering inevitably led through his own suffering, to death. They did call his truth subversive, heretical, blasphemous. They denounced his works of healing and compassion as deeds of the devil. Oh how he suffered! Even Jesus' best friends praised him for the wrong reasons, then betrayed, denied, and forsook him. He sweated blood as he asked in his heart why men chose to be so perverse and do such cruel things to one another and to him. It could have been so different. His last hours were utter humiliation, rejection, and agony. He has rightly been called the Man of Sorrows. I usually think of his wonderful ministry of teaching, healing, and helping as being full of beauty, goodness, and power. But he felt such deep compassion for the suffering people whom he served, that to him his ministry must have been continuous suffering. The Creed sums up his thirty-three years in one phrase, "suffered under Pontius Pilate." What an insight!

Whatever path of suffering may lie ahead for me, Jesus has explored it right down to the end. And he kept his faith! Jesus never spared himself any kind of suffering that I may ever have to face. Not once did he pull a miracle to get himself off the hook. I'll never be able to say that he doesn't understand what I'm going through.

suffered . . .

Jesus' suffering had depths to it that I shall never fully understand. As an artist suffers when vandals destroy his work, so God must suffer while men wreck his world. But God's heart aches mostly for the *wreckers* who have cheated and ruined themselves. God suffers when we suffer. When I hurt someone, God winces. As an erupting volcano brings to light the ageless, deep, hot core of the earth, so Jesus' suffering gave us a glimpse of the perpetual suffering of God's "eternal cross." The Lamb of God was slain "before the foundation of the world." Most of my life I've been making God's life hell! All along, I've been God's problem of suffering, and yet I've been asking him to explain to me the problem of suffering!

It's hard to understand why he lets us all go on this way. Mankind couldn't have been more cruel and heartless to him than that Calvary time. Why did he take all that torturous treatment rather than strike us down? He said he had forgiven us! He had the power right then to wipe us off the face of the earth, but he did nothing. He really must have forgiven us! He certainly postponed judgment. Mankind lives from day to day under God's mercy. The cross stands in history like a great dam up in the mountains, holding back the waters of doom that might have roared down upon us and our frail little fripperies. God chose to suffer in himself rather than to smash us.

But why did he choose to forgive us? Because he loves us? There may be more to it than even that. To make a world where love and goodness would have any value, God had to leave men free to hate and destroy —which they did in spite of laws, governments, and teachers. Yet God did not move to disarm them or reduce them to will-less, harmless robots. None of the suffering caused by human sin could have happened if God had not decided to make and maintain a world of free men. Once I heard a man say bitterly, "God should be punished for making such a world as this! He should be made to come down here and suffer what we have to suffer." He had forgotten that God *has* come already in Jesus and exposed himself to the terrible abuse of human freedom. God has taken responsibility for our woes, accepting personally the consequences of the kind of world he had created. *He* suffered for *our* sins, although we are the ones who are guilty, not he. He withheld judgment and passed no sentence on us. We are still free to be ourselves in these days of grace.

By coming in Jesus, God gave us the means to make our ways and world a delight instead of the same old torture. He made his own life available to us, to rescue us from the misery of sin and death. But when a rescuer swims out with a lifeline to seamen on a battered wreck, he must suffer through the same pounding seas that roar over the seamen. God in Christ was suffering

74

as he brought through to us what we needed to save us from ruin. Why did Jesus suffer? In two words—for me!

suffered under Pontius Pilate

This man Pilate was not merely a private individual. He was the representative of the vast system of Roman law and power. Insofar as law is a restraint upon reckless evildoers it reduces human suffering considerably. Jesus recognized Pilate's office as one of God's gifts to the world and submitted to his judgment. But on the other hand, the Roman system, like all human systems, could cause a great deal of suffering. Power can always be abused and laws can always be made to work for the unscrupulous. Pontius Pilate was interested mostly in his own future in the system. The Jewish enemies of Jesus' truth and love could cause Pilate a lot of trouble, so he gave in to their pressure. He sent the best of us to our worst kind of death. Some judge! Pontius Pilate therefore stands for the inherent weaknesses and dreadful possibilities that lie within all human organizations. None of them is worthy of ultimate worship and absolute loyalty. If human systems are to fulfill the place God intended for them in history, they must always be open to the Word of God in Christ. In Pontius Pilate the Roman and Jewish systems rejected

Christ. They were therefore rejected by God. All systems that reject his truth and compassion are doomed. They have no future. Pilate thought that he was condemning Jesus, but he had only succeeded in condemning himself and his system. All efforts to do away with Jesus came to nothing, for he rose from the dead forever.

The Spirit of the Lord is still at work in his world. He uses the words and lives of his servants to change others so that they become more like Jesus. He can transform the Pontius Pilates. He can create new systems which are nearer to what he has ever hoped for. Whatever my post in society may be, if Christ's Spirit shines out from me, the Lord works among my associates. Some will be won to his truth and love and become fellow workers with me for God's kingdom of peace. Others may turn on me as they turned in fury upon Jesus. Then I, too, shall learn what it is to "suffer under Pontius Pilate." But I must be willing, for the sake of suffering men and my suffering God, to suffer with and for Christ. There is a fellowship of Christ's suffering.

The world which God loves cannot come to the end of its suffering unless people begin to live in Christ's truth and love. Somebody's got to live the Christ-life in the midst of men if they're going to get caught up by him. Somebody's got to put himself out for others. Somebody's got to absorb the world's violence and halt the blow-for-blow retaliation that leads only to destruction. When he calls me to suffer in his name, to return good for evil, he has called me to the highest possible privilege—the opportunity of having my life really count in making something come true of God's dream of peace for his suffering world. He who undertakes to suffer willingly for the Lord has tasted the joy of life's ultimate victory.

was crucified . . .

I believe that Jesus Christ was God come in the flesh to rescue mankind. Obviously this was not what most men of Jesus' times believed. Jesus was crucified. The Jewish religion, like Roman law and Greek culture, had no place for him. But Jesus cared too much to hold his peace or go quietly away. So they ousted him. They made Jesus haul a heavy cross well outside the wall of their holy city and up a hill. There they spread him out on the wood and spiked him to it by his hands and feet. When they had heaved up the cross into its socket in the rock, they gaped in glee at their handiwork. Until he died he hung up there in the sky in naked agony—neither on the earth nor in heaven but in no-man's-land, totally rejected and utterly accursed. Jesus was not killed from ambush by a single assassin. Nor was he lynched by a handful of hotheads. He was repudiated officially and entirely by his society and culture. They simply crossed him out for what they regarded as good and sufficient reasons.

Religious, respectable men crucified Jesus. They were our kind of people. We got most of our basic ideas about justice and mercy, faith and reason, virtue and righteousness from them. They were no breed of monsters, but well-educated, responsible men who herded Jesus to that horrible cross. Yet those highly religious, highly respectable men spawned a deed so foul that the very earth under their feet shuddered for shame, and the bright sun hid its face from the sight of them. But God in his mercy did not scrape those wretches from the earth and destroy them. If the best of us deserved nothing but destruction, what about the rest of us? Can I be sure that I would never be capable of such a horrible deed? Under certain conditions I might be capable of anything. Although God usually has me pretty well in hand through the Spirit of Christ and the controls of civilization, every so often something ugly and destructive boils up in me and in every man—something bent on destroying the work of God.

There is a destroyer, a voracious parasite in God's garden—this world. God always had to work to keep his garden. He created his world in the midst of nothingness, and nothingness was in the midst of it. Energy always tends to dart off into the emptiness like air rushing into a vacuum. The nameless realm of nothingness sucks off the substance of my candle through its flame until there is nothing at all left of it. Candles always burn *down*. Finally the wax is gone, the light is gone, and the heat currents die away into the cold. Men can never bring this lost energy back together again to remake the candle. While I'm trying to move something, there's something busy dragging it down to a dead stop. This destroyer attacks even the everlasting hills, and tears at our houses and tombstones until they crumble and vanish away. Everything that lives eventually loses its life to this deadly cosmic leech, this unseen vampire— nothingness, the destroyer. To be a creature is to be embattled and besieged. The moment God creates something, its enemy is there on its doorstep. Everything in God's creation is vulnerable to this sinister destroyer, this ancient quicksand that seeks to swallow up God's world. Good Lord, deliver me!

was crucified . . .

This is a perishing world, always threatened with destruction by the uncreated realm of nothingness. All light and existence would long since have disappeared if it had not been for the inexhaustible creative resources of God. All unity would have disintegrated ages ago if God had not held his world together, or if God had not cared. We men live every moment out of the riches and might and love of God.

The enemy of God's world is in us men. How we labor under the destroyer! Life's a continuous struggle against a downward drag. I get tired when doing good —or doing anything at all, for that matter. My enthusiasms wane, and my spirits droop, and I settle for the easy thing—the long coast downhill. I spend most of my time and energy in dealing with my own pressing problems. Other people become a burden and a threat to me. Something sullen and untamed in me rises up against anyone who bothers me, even God. Fine respectable men were relieved when Jesus was crucified. They had problems enough of their own without the ones he was raising. That's what can happen to men who are meant to show forth the image of God's holy love. Permeated through and through by God's ancient enemy, we too become enemies of God's Son and crucify him. The human race has been learning how to handle disease and starvation and how to avoid violence. But how do we deactivate the destroyer in the best of us? God help us! God help me!

In a way I'm like a seafarer adrift in a leaky old boat. The hull barely manages to keep the death dealing seawater away from me. But that saltwater keeps eating away at the boat and seeping into it. I never know when or where it will break in next to menace me. Day after day I spend in just plugging leaks. But the thing that scares me is that sometimes I suspect that the "seawater" madness has soaked into me too. I get so furious at the confounded old tub that someday I may not be able to keep from stomping my foot right through its decadent planking. The boat—my God-given lot in life—is my life's shield and resource, but sometimes I hate it, I hate it, I hate it! My prison and torturer! I could crucify it! The Creator's ancient enemy is my enemy too. But the enemy is part of myself, part of my own creaturely, perishing nature.

God in his heaven has eternal life. The destroyer cannot so much as scratch him. God is the wellspring of creativity. His reservoir cannot be drained dry. But the world which God made is not an eternal world. It is a perishing world. Though it often shines with glints of God's glory, they quickly dim and die out. There is a cosmic thief who is always making off with God's jewels. Moments of time filled with God's holy love, moments of sacrifice for others, moments of truth and compassion, moments of faith and hope—these are God's own jewels. For these the world was made. But the destroyer quickly drags them down to oblivion. How can God get back his own? He was able to regain his lost treasures by letting himself be dragged down to where they are. He was crucified, dead, buried, and descended to the realm of the dead.

was crucified, dead . . .

From all eternity God was preparing to seek out his treasure for safekeeping forever. Someone would have to go down into the created world, and on down into the dim regions of the past, to seek and to save what might otherwise be lost. Man as a creature was at best a leaky boat, and the cargo was so precious.

Only God himself was unsinkable. Man could not be made into a God, because a "really-truly" God cannot be made. But the Almighty *could* contain himself within thingy limits and shrink his powers as far as necessary to dwell in a human frame. This he did. The Son of God was born of the Virgin Mary. As Jesus of Nazareth he lived a man's life, tempted and tried by all the powers of darkness, by the destroyer. But this man, unlike the others, did not let down his guard. He never backed away from the truth about his fellowmen, yet people never became an unbearable burden to him. Faithful to reality and full of compassion, Jesus shone with God's holy love whenever he made his decisions and put them into action. This was man as he was meant to be.

But could Jesus face total rejection and death, yet still hold on to his childlike trust that God was worthy and winning? If the world fell in on him, would he still say, "Thy will, not mine, be done"? How far down would Jesus' faith and loyalty last? The dark destroyer was turned loose on him. The world he had shared in creating was hurled against him. His fellowmen went at him with ropes, chains, whips, hammers, nails, and spittle. He was crucified. The earth never lifted a finger to help him, and the last wisp of the presence of heaven departed. On the cross the destroyer tightened his grip to strangle the life out of Jesus. But still he prayed for his enemies, looked out for his mother, and comforted a dying thief! The God-man was on his own now, operating at a single manpower, facing alone the full force of the age-old enemy of all creation. Would this one of us make it to the highest height of God's hope for men and become the means of delivering us all from the destroyer? Out of the darkness around that cross Jesus gave a loud cry of supreme trust: "Father, into thy hands I commit my spirit." Then he bowed his head and breathed his last. Jesus was dead. The destroyer had dragged him down to death like all others. But he had been true to God to the very end.

It had been a long road down. The Son of God had died to his heavenly glory in order to become a perishing man whose living is really a continuous process of dying. My life right now is continually becoming my past—going, going, almost gone, ever dimmer and dimmer. Jesus also died daily to himself. He was so concerned about helping his fellow sufferers that he forgot about striving for righteousness in and for himself. He thus became splendidly and totally right in the sight of God, even to his last breath on the cross. Here was the perfect earthly image of God and his selfless love. By taking up his cross daily and dying to himself for the sake of God and men, Jesus had been fighting off the destroyer whose sting shows up as sin and ends in death. Even though he had never borne sin marks, Jesus now was dead.

. . . dead, and buried;
he descended into hell

All the way through his dying, Jesus had trusted in God and in the power of truth and love, no matter what the cost to himself. At last one man had entirely measured up to God's dream. Jesus was altogether worthy of everlasting trust and eternal life. He was just the one to become the Savior of all of God's treasures. Although the destroyer's attack on Jesus had left him hanging dead upon the cross, he was utterly victorious in the sight of God. That day the joy bells rang in heaven, and the celebration hasn't ceased yet even on earth! "As often as you eat this bread and drink the cup, you proclaim the Lord's death until he comes."

Jesus was buried. Some brave and charitable men laid what was left of him in a tomb. When the authorities sealed up the big stone door, Jesus' enemies gloated. That troubler had been disposed of at last. Good riddance to bad rubbish! But this world isn't big enough to bury the fact that a Jesus had lived in it. The word of his mouth and the word of his deeds could not be buried as easily as his body.

Jesus' downward descent from the eternal fullness of God did not stop with the cross and the tomb. He went right on down in the perishing as far as he could go without ceasing to exist—right to the bottom of being.

Before Christ's time the breakup of a man continued as long as a vestige of power remained of him, until all that was left of him was like a shadow cast by a dim light on a dark wall. The abode of the departed was sheol to the Jews, hades to the Greeks. The Anglo-Saxon word "hell" stood for a place of torture. The English had no equivalent word or idea for the abode of the dead, so the word "hell" was used to translate both the abode of the dead and the different idea of a place of torture. "Hell" stands in the Creed nevertheless for an uncanny realm of perpetual perishing and disintegration. Hell was a vague frontier borderland between the uttermost reach of God's creativity and the silent abyss of sheer nothingness. It was where the lives of men ebb to their lowest and are suspended in a state of weightlessness, as it were. Into this dissolving obscurity all the past had passed on its way out.

I believe that Jesus, too, descended into hell. He endured the full pangs and bitterness of death. Whatever may be involved in dying, in any realms beyond our sight, Jesus underwent that, too. Wherever any of the departed ever got to, the Lord has gone to them. There is no forgotten corner of creation, no hidden crevasse or sunken depth into which he has not penetrated to recover the lost. We'll never know what our Lord went through as he let himself go down, down as far as down goes. If I am in him, I shall never experience what it is to descend into hell. He died my deepest death for me.

the third day he rose again from the dead

Death had taken all men throughout the ages. Around every living person the shadow of death always circled like that of a hovering vulture. Eventually every man would die and stay dead. It didn't matter whether or not he was bad or good, ignorant or skilled and learned, ugly or handsome, hated or beloved, ordinary or famous and creative. The great destroyer devoured all men alike and dragged them down toward nothingness. Men said, Why make an effort to be good? Why bother to learn? Why try to build things up? Life was meaningless and futile. If there are any gods, they must either be weaklings or cruel monsters. Men sometimes dreamed of a life after death. They wanted to keep on living as they were at their prime or better. They worked up reasons for believing that it would be so, but those few shaky arguments were only mere straws of hope to be clutched at by desperate, dying waifs. As far as anyone could see for sure, the world was mostly an immense graveyard. Every news story ended with the same old obituary notice.

I am now about to write once again the most important words that have ever been written by anyone anywhere anytime. I'd like to write them in mountain-sized letters of blazing ink right across the heavens. I'd like to finish with an exclamation mark that would sound like an H-bomb going off and shoot up like a space rocket. *Christ is risen!* The discovery of America, the invention of electronic voices, space flights and atomic power belong in the back pages of the human story when rated with the best news ever: death has been conquered!

The news that Christ had risen burst into this deathly world like a flaming comet. Here was a headline to end all headlines. The universal reign of death had been broken at last by a remarkable man named Jesus. This man had died—really died—his enemies had seen to that. But he had come back from the realm of the dead to the land of the living. He had moved among his former friends for some weeks. Then he had somehow moved beyond them into a higher kind of existence. Jesus' conquest of death was most significant, for what has happened in the case of one man can possibly happen again with others. Out of the news of this victory the most glorious hope was born, and a faith that has transformed human living.

When I get discouraged because the work I'm trying to do in the name of the Lord hasn't yet blossomed, I have to take a new hold on my faith. Eventually God will have his way. Maybe not today or tomorrow, but the day will come nevertheless. After the dark hours there will come the third day! After the silence, after the suspense, on the third day, God will honor his word. Christ's life will stir where I have buried it in other men's hearts. The resurrection will go on and on until all that God values in this world has been gathered safely in.

... *he rose again from the dead*

The evidence for Christ's resurrection lies all around me in things that can be traced away back through history to find their meaning and explanation in the reality of Christ's rising.

The Lord's Day, Sunday, the first day of the week, became a special day of worship for the Jewish disciples, who had always emphasized the seventh day according to the fourth commandment. Only a tremendous event like the resurrection could have driven them to change their emphasis. We follow their lead and still observe the Lord's Day.

The Christian church, which has always been an utterly unique thing among the religions of the world, could neither have begun nor spread without the resurrection. This most remarkable social phenomenon of all time could not be sensibly or satisfactorily explained if Jesus did not rise from the dead. The resurrection was central in the church's message from the beginning, well before the Gospel stories about the risen Jesus were written. The apostles were respected as authorities because they were the witnesses of the resurrection. It was Christ's rising that turned those beaten, cowardly disciples into brave proclaimers of the resurrection, though their message upset every system of human thinking. They risked dying for their message because their resurrection-Lord could rescue them even in death. They went out into the world with everything to lose and nothing to gain, just to tell the world that Christ was risen. My church would not be here today if Jesus had not risen.

The Lord's Supper, beginning in the earliest church, has always told of a Lord who died with a broken body and shed blood. But the Supper is to be served "until he comes." The one who was dead must be alive if we are to have communion with him and if he is to return. The Lord's Supper is another witness to the resurrection.

Baptism into the Lord's death and resurrection would never have begun in the early church if Christ had not risen. John's baptism would have been enough. Only after he had risen did Jesus command his disciples to baptize.

The cross, like a gallows, was originally the sign of disgrace, defeat, and death. Because Christ arose it came to be a symbol of triumphant victory and life. So it will ever be.

The letters of Saul of Tarsus tell how he persecuted Christians but became convinced that Christ had risen. He collected a list of the times the risen Jesus had reappeared to his followers (I Cor. 15). As Paul, the missionary, he outpreached and outwrote the apostles on the subject of the resurrection, years before the

Gospels were written. His writings, even if taken merely as historical documents, are a testimony to Jesus' rising by one of Christ's former enemies.

The Gospels with Jesus' big claims and big promises would neither have been written nor preserved if Jesus had not risen. His disillusioned followers would have debunked him instead of proclaiming him Lord of all. The New Testament does not and cannot explain the resurrection. But the resurrection certainly explains the existence of the New Testament.

I believe that Jesus rose from the dead. Theories which try to explain away the resurrection always contradict one another and are altogether unfounded and inadequate. Christ's resurrection is like a spear pointed at the stubborn heart of an unbeliever.

. . . he rose again from the dead

The resurrection spotlighted Jesus. His conquest of death made the world sit up and take notice. What Jesus had taught had not really been unique, except in what he had said about himself. He had made certain bold claims that only God could rightfully make. But Jesus' death on the cross undermined those claims so completely that, if he had stayed dead, the world would have heard no more of him. It was because Jesus rose from the dead that thinking men had to take a new look at his claims. This Jesus who had conquered death either possessed superhuman power or enjoyed the special favor of a superhuman power. If men were not prepared to admit that Jesus himself was God, it at least seemed clear that God had thoroughly endorsed all that Jesus had said and done. But Jesus had led people to believe that he was the Son of God. Then God had agreed that that's exactly who he was. By bringing Jesus back from the dead, God had declared, clearly and resoundingly, "This is my beloved Son, with whom I am well pleased; listen to him!" God himself had overruled the judgment of the Jew's supreme court and Rome's Pilate.

God had certified that Jesus had been telling the truth and living it. From henceforth men would know whom to believe and how they should be living. No need to flounder around among the world's religious opinions wondering which of them is trustworthy! They could trust Jesus and believe in his belief. God did! This meant that at last men had some reliable knowledge about what God is like. God had revealed himself by what he had approved. There was no need to wonder further about what is really right to do and what is wrong. By raising Jesus from the dead, God had established Jesus' kind of living as the standard by which all men's actions are to be judged. No matter what men may think about ethical questions, Jesus is what God thinks is right. What is truly Christlike cannot be wrong.

The resurrection gave authority to Jesus' words and

deeds. Men sought out the words which this most important person had spoken and they retold the story of what he had done. In so doing they stumbled upon the answer to the problem of how to enable men to live Christlike lives. They found that there was still enough personal power left in the words of Jesus to start a "resurrection" wherever they were heard. Reading Jesus' words from New Testament writings or hearing them from the lips of preachers was like hearing Jesus himself speak. Jesus himself was in his words and his Spirit accompanied his words with power to transform lives. The word of Christ is Christ. Whoever receives Jesus' words receives the Lord himself, even in the twentieth century. His words get under peoples' skins and into their blood, as it were. Like seeds, his words grow within our lives and reproduce in us the kind of living from which they came: the life of Christ. The church has been sent into the world bearing the seed to be planted everywhere. The word of Christ is the means of continuing the resurrection of a body of Christ in this world. The Scriptures not only share in the authority of the risen Christ; they are the outreach of his personal power.

. . . he rose again from the dead

The heart center of Christianity is the resurrection of Christ. There is a road to every important point of Christian faith and life from the resurrection. Every other doctrine depends upon this for its foundation. Without the resurrection the whole Christian structure falls apart and tumbles in ruins. Everything in the Creed before "he rose from the dead" simply leads up to this. And everything that follows it follows from it. I cannot overemphasize the place of the resurrection in my faith. Without this I would have nothing significant to say. For me the resurrection explains and grounds everything Christian. It explains why Christianity is quite different from every other religion. It even explains me.

A new age had begun. An entirely new kind of being had appeared in this perishing world. Jesus had been thoroughly part of our doomed, creaturely human race. But while in our flesh, he had succeeded in being willingly, lovingly, and entirely at one with God. What the Creator had desired for every man had been realized in history at least once. The man Jesus could be trusted forever with all the powers of God. The Almighty therefore brought him back out of the power of death to live eternally and to wield all power in heaven and on earth. The risen Lord could move equally well in the realm of the Creator and in the realm of the creatures. Locked doors, long distances, and fixed times were no longer barriers to him.

This new kind of being made possible the rescue of God's creaturely treasures even out of past history and the abode of the dead. It also made possible the beginning and building of a new world both here and hereafter. The risen Lord could make his way even into the lives of perishing and perverse people. He could relive in them something of his victorious life. They would share in his resurrection and eternal life. Since the risen Lord had bridged the gap between the creatures and the Creator and could move in both directions, he could do something about bringing estranged sinners together with the Holy God. When the Lord joined sinful men to God, as the spokes of a wheel join the rim to the hub, also and at the same time he joined men to one another through himself. This created the Christian church, which consists of those men who are at one with God and one another through the work of the risen Christ. And who can tell of all the blessings which the church has brought to mankind? The resurrection of Jesus thus brought about the most important change ever in the human situation. A new age had dawned with the resurrection and a whole new world could begin.

he ascended . . .

The Creed tells a story about the Son of God descending from heaven to this earth, then to the depths of death, returning here again, only to ascend once more into heaven. It assumes the existence of "heaven" and "hell" or "hades." These "places" do not appear anywhere in the world view of our times. In biblical times, however, heaven was up there beyond the skies, and hell was down there in the bowels of the earth where all the graves joined up to form a great gloomy underground cavern. People's imaginations had free play in furnishing details about the population and geography of these unseen realms. While I may not be able to accept much of the quaint imagery I have inherited from yesteryear, I still find it necessary to believe in some "higher" world and "lower" world, using "higher" and "lower" in nongeographical senses. Everybody knows what I mean when I speak of higher prices or a lower I.Q., of higher-ups or low-lifers. Until all things are absolutely equalized so that each thing is identical with everything else, we shall go on arranging them in scales of value and quality from high to low.

This being so, the essential meaning of the story of Christ's epic journey from heaven to hell and back can be retained without being involved in any unacceptable imagery from an obsolete world view. In the world around me, there are obviously higher and lower forms of life. Human beings have a greater range of possibilities and much higher powers than the lesser animals. Plants are more limited still, and inorganic substances can do practically nothing by themselves. Now where are the upper and lower ends of this scale of being? How far down does existence go before it ceases to exist at all? When does light peter out into darkness, and sound become silence, and the last movement become still? In his prime a man can live with all the stops open on the wonderful instrument of his human existence. But eventually his powers decline through illness, old age, and the disintegration of death. He continues to perish physically and psychically until only the merest trace of his existence is left. This lowest state of being, whatever it may be, is what I mean by hades, or hell.

Working up the scale of being in the opposite and ascending direction, we move up to higher possibilities for human life. Who can tell how far up we can go? Light waves may exist and vibrate, but it takes something higher than light waves to *see* light and the things that light reveals. There is a realm yet higher than seeing: the realm of thinking about things. And higher than that . . . ? I know that there are sounds my ears cannot hear and light my eyes cannot see. Beyond the reach of my present powers there likely is an undetectable realm with ranges and kinds of being which I cannot as yet begin to conceive. Here there may be certain kinds of creatures (angels?) which are quite at home in this higher world, whose natures nobody would now understand. Such possible higher states of being beyond the edge of our map are what I mean by heaven. Heaven may be all about me, even in me, for all I know, but it is still out of reach. In heaven, God always has his own way because it is the highest and best way.

Using heaven and hell in these senses, the descent and ascent of Christ can become meaningful to a modern mind.

he ascended into heaven

The story contained in the Creed consists of two basic movements, first descending then ascending. The Son of God went down to become also the Son of man. His descent began in the glory of the Father Almighty. God's eternal Son laid aside his garments of light and his powers, and came to be part of our blighted, untoward, earthborn race. As Jesus of Nazareth, he suffered at men's hands, was crucified, died, and was buried. Down, down he went, even into hell, the abode of the past and the dead. He had plunged from the highest heaven to the depths of death, through the whole range of existence, right to the very bottom of being.

But even at the lowest ebb of his powers, the light that was in him could not be put out by the very deepest darkness. God at his weakest survived and defeated the full force of the destroyer which had always dragged down everything he had created.

Then began the second movement of the Creed—the ascension of Christ as the Son of both God and man. This ascending movement of the victorious Lord began right in the abode of the dead. What took place there can only be described by sanctified imagination. At this phase of Christ's ascension, paradise came into being, for his victory over death affected even the con-

97

dition of the faithful dead, bringing them into fuller life, security, and peace.

Next, Jesus returned to become part of our world again. What we call his resurrection is really the second phase of his ascension. He took up his bodily nature again, along with all his human powers, plus a portion of his divine powers. The risen Jesus was the same, and yet very different, as his humanity was being glorified. He appeared from time to time among his old companions for some weeks. He helped them to recall what he had formerly said and done, and all of it took on new meaning in the light of his resurrection. The Lord promised to give his personal power to the words of his disciples if they would go out as apostles to tell the world all the good news about him.

But there was to be yet another and final phase of Jesus' ascension. One morning when they were all walking up the hill toward Bethany, Jesus turned and raised his hands. Even as he was blessing them, he began to move away from them—out of focus somehow—and they lost sight of him as in a shimmering cloud. That was no mere mist of water vapor. Men had seen that cloud before. It was that sign of the presence of God which had led the Israelites through the wilderness— the same cloud that had come down upon the Mount of Transfiguration. The apostles understood at once that their Lord and Master had gone back to his Father and home—as quietly as he had come into this world thirty-three years before. His human qualities had gone along with him into heaven as he took up once again

the full powers of God. When Jesus disappeared as a
bodily presence from this world, he took on a way of
existing that is quite different from ours, with powers
and possibilities that we can't even imagine. But his
going opened a door into heaven for us men. It is now
possible for beings from the abode of the dead and
from this world, as well as heaven, to come to be forever with God. All this was accomplished by the three
phases of the ascension of Christ.

he ascended into heaven

When the Son of God had been reduced to next to
nothing at all in the realm of the dead, it was quite
clear that death could not put out the last spark of him,
even at his weakest. As a man, Jesus had been entirely
faithful right to the end, trusting in God to the uttermost. God was now ready to make a new beginning with
the human race and all his created world. God and man
could now be together in a new way with all the endless
possibilities of eternal life.

That last dim ember of God, not quite gone out,
began to glow again in the realm of the dead. Jesus
began to take to himself again the powers of the Son
of man and the Son of God. His ascension commenced.

The Spirit of Jesus stood forth in splendid radiance.
All around, the shadows disappeared before the light

of the Lord of life. Soon the word of God's new world-in-the-making was rolling throughout the long caverns of the days that were past and the men who were gone. The faint vestiges of the faithful people of God, who had once received with joy the promise of a coming deliverer, began to respond to the word that sought them out. Perhaps also those others who, though they had never heard the promise God had made to Israel, had been seriously faithful to such truth as they had. Though they were dead, they began to live. As one piano echoes the tone of another, the dead came forth in answer to Christ's call. His "jewels" began to flash back to him his own glorious light. The Son of God ransacked the ancient stronghold of death for men of old who were the rightful treasures of God. The liberated captives of death streamed up out of their dungeons to pledge their devotion to their Lord. He threw open the gates of hell from the inside and led his people out of their perpetual perishing. A fair and pleasant land began to spread before them as they came. He was preparing a place for them which he called paradise.

Who can describe the wonder of that new realm, full of the light of the Savior's presence, where they were to await the time of the fulfillment of all things! There they wait in the full certainty of hope and in the sweetest of peace. There is no more perishing for them, for there is a great gulf fixed between them and the deadly past. For them there is only the blissful present with Christ and the anticipation of a still more wonderful future. The believing thief who died beside Jesus came into paradise with Jesus the very first day as promised. And thither go all our blessed dead who die today in the Lord. With him in life, they continue with him in death.

Christ's power successfully penetrated the whole spread of God's world. Even the gates of hell could not stand in his way, for he has the keys of death and hell. He was able to save to the uttermost. Because Jesus began his ascent from the deepest depths of death, I believe in paradise.

he ascended . . .

Christ began his ascending in this physical world of ours after three days' work among the dead. He was not satisfied to remain a disembodied spirit. He didn't leave his fleshly corpse behind him in the tomb. He didn't discard his broken body as vile, useless, irrelevant, or unimportant. Everything in this whole world was destined to ascend along with him. So he took up even the bodily side of his human nature into the new kind of being. His body was transposed, as it were, into a higher key. The risen Christ was neither a mere ghost nor a revived corpse, one who would sometime die again. In his resurrection and for days afterward Christ was being glorified, becoming a spiritual body. He was still entirely the same person whom his disciples had formerly known. His voice carried the same wonderful overtones of love for them. After a miserable night's unsuccessful fishing, he had a nice hot breakfast ready on the shore for his wet, tired disciples. Jesus' hands still bore the scars of the nails, which he would wear forever, the sign of his willingness to suffer for those he loves. But his bodily presence had already changed so remarkably that they would hardly have known him. Doors could no longer shut out his body, although that body still had substance. He could appear anywhere anytime, then disappear at will. Jesus knew that Thomas had blurted out his doubts, even though Thomas had no idea that he was present at the time. He was ascending to another order of being—as when the dead, poisonous stuff in garden soil is taken up into the tissues of a living plant with its higher functions of growth and beauty and fruitfulness. Dead plants, which are not me but only my food, become part of the living *me* after I eat them. The plants then share in what I think is a more interesting and higher kind of existence. What is dead can thus obviously come to life. It is commonplace now to use dead serum from a blood bank for transfusions. Some of the blind may see again by engrafted parts of dead men's eyes. No one can know for sure that either resurrection or ascension is utterly *impossible*. In any case, the last phases of the resurrection and ascension of Jesus were utterly unique. Scientific laws cannot be made about the unique, nor have we ideas capable of dealing with what is an entirely different kind of being. When I say that Jesus ascended into the highest, I mean that he changed into a far less limited order of being. Once he was visible; now he is invisible. Formerly Jesus was confined to a single place at a certain time in this world. Now he can operate anytime, anywhere, at any level of being right up to the highest heaven. Hitherto his disciples had been following Jesus, learning from their teacher. From now on they would be calling everybody together to worship him and to share in his eternal and victorious life.

he ascended . . .

Jesus' passage into heaven was important to him in many ways. He had finished the preparatory work which God had given him to do. God's vanishing treasures of human life had been safely gathered together in paradise. Eternally victorious life had been made available for men. A process of ascension had been begun which would eventually involve everything in the whole world. Jesus' mission had been a success. He had survived the greatest adventure ever and his exploit had come off with honor. The Son of God returned as a scarred but conquering hero and presented his work to God. Heaven heard it being accepted and attested with the great "Well done!" Now the Son was home again where he had always belonged. It was good to be home. But yet there was something altogether strange about it. For the human side of him, this coming into heaven was entirely new. It was the first time anyone who had been flesh and blood had ever passed this way. Christ was a pioneer, and there was a delight to it like making the first tracks in newfallen snow or opening up a new continent. He knew that where he had come others now might follow. God had united himself with something of mankind forever. If man had lost his image of God, God himself had taken on the image of man in Christ. From this fact the human race has gained its highest dignity.

Something of me is already with the ascended Christ in glory. If Christ is in me and I am in Christ, then something of me is not entirely of the earth, earthy. My true life is hidden with Christ in God. My life in this world may be sick or weak, but whatever is of Christ in me is vigorous and strong, rooted in heaven. My human life is easily temptable, but the Christlife in me resists temptation and gives me my highest conscience. I may get upset and discouraged, but only if I forget that in the Ascended One I have peace and joy. The anchor of my little earthly boat reaches deep into the unseen and holds fast in the realm of God. Although I may drift around in circles, the Christ in me will always hold me near to the things that are really important. Just because I'm anchored in heaven, however, I can't expect to escape entirely this world's winds and waves. I may be tossed about by the storms, yet I know that my boat will never be wrecked on the rocks.

My life's treasure is firmly held in his hands. And where my treasure is, there my heart is also.

Christ's ascension brought him nearer to us. When I carry a light ahead of me through a crowd without lights, most of the people remain in the shadows. But when I hold my light high, all of the others get some of the light. When the sun shines from on high at noon, everything beneath it is lighted up. As long as Jesus was merely a man in one place at a time, he could not be with everyone at once. But free from our limitations, having ascended into heaven, he could be with each one of us always. From highest heaven he can fill all things with himself and thus bring them to their fulfillment. The sun may be ninety-three million miles away, but its light, heat, and gravitational attraction are right here with us. So, though Christ may be bodily absent, he is nevertheless very present in his Spirit, word, sacraments, and church. He is not only in heaven. He is also a real presence on earth and in paradise. The ascended Christ bridges the ages and the ends of the universe.

he ascended into heaven

Jesus' ascension into the highest from the depths was the first instance of a new kind of being: creature style, but eternal in life. Others of the human race would soon be able to take on the beginnings of this higher life, with hope of entering eventually into its fullness. Christ had promised this to his followers and he still wants it for them. He is still alive, with all power, and I believe that he has kept and will continue to keep his promises. I have already received some first installments of his wonderful life. The rest will come to me in due time. But if it were not for my ascended Lord, I would not have any real basis for a reasonable hope of a life worth living after my death.

Deep within me, day by day, I feel the upward calling of God in Christ Jesus. It is as if I were caught up in a great heavenward current which was started by the ascension of Jesus. This upward-tending stream has ever since been raising the quality of human life. The full meaning of the ascension of the Lord is seen in the movement of God's world toward the fulfillment of its Creator's eternal purpose. All things in this world are meant to be gathered together somehow, someday, in the oneness of the Son of God's glorified body, so that he may be all in all. All treasures that came into being in God's great workshop of history must be saved, transformed, and put together like the pieces of a cosmic puzzle. Only then will the Lord's resurrection and ascension be completed in a new heaven and a new earth. Anyone who ever shared in the new being of Christ will find place and meaning. After the harvest will come the feast. The full significance of Christ will appear when all that was part of him has finally been assembled together and glorified. We shall see all of him as he is, and we shall be like him. Beholding the lines of his restored creation, the Lord God will stretch out his arms to us all and cry out in joy to all before him, "My Son! My Son! Man!" The Christlike men of that new world will freely and willingly live for God and one another, moving together from glory to glory. Such is the hope which arises for us from Christ's ascension.

If his ascension is so important, the church should make more of it. The Christ of past history will always be the basis of Christian teaching, of course. We cannot help but make a great deal of his birth, life, death, and resurrection. But we also need to maintain vividly our consciousness of the living Christ, the Christ of experience, the Christ of heaven, the Christ of the present and of the future. When we lose the ascended Christ, we lose our purpose, our strength, and our hope. Christmas and Easter have become so cluttered up by commercialism and worthless pagan garbage that these holy seasons have become next to useless for Christian purposes. But as yet no public splurge or busy rush occurs at Ascensiontide. The papers scarcely mention the ascension. Neither do the churches! Yet all the basic values of the incarnation and the resurrection are gathered up in the ascension. It contains the climax of everything we want to say about Jesus at those other seasons.

and sitteth on the right hand of God . . .

Christ has not abandoned this world, even though he has ascended and is no longer visibly present. He still operates through Christians and the church although his personal center is in heaven. Because he has been working in his church, I am writing these words and you are reading them. Yet I believe that there is very much more to Christ than I am now able to know of him by his presence here in this world. He holds the highest possible position at the master control center of the universe. That's what I mean when I say: He sitteth on the right hand of God.

Most men do their work with their right hand. Someone who is capable of sharing my work, who has put himself at my disposal and is willing to carry out my wishes, is my "right-hand man." The right hand is the place of power, the place of honor, the station of faithful friends and trusted counselors. Now I don't imagine that God has sides with arms and hands, but I know that his "throne" is the hub of all power in heaven and on earth. I believe that the one nearest to this center of things is Jesus Christ. He is God's right-hand man. Christ is in on all the secret counsels of God. God's program and Christ's continuing activity fit together perfectly. One of our human race is in such intimate communion with the Father, so at one with the Almighty, that he in effect presides over the outcome of future history. Whatever men may think that God is like, Christians know that God's world is not merely a mindless machine run by a pitiless impersonal power. The world is in the hands of the most wonderful person I could ever imagine, one who possesses at least the highest human qualities that men have ever known. That person is Jesus Christ, who is the Lord of all.

Christ sits to serve our best interests and those of God. He sits like a judge or a parliament, like a consultant or an advocate. He has the power to handle things nicely and calmly from where he is. The Christ who once died for us still lives for us and is performing a heavenly ministry on our behalf. As long as Jesus is right there at the center of things, we know that God is sticking by his dream for mankind. Beholding Jesus, he still has hope for the rest of us. God has not given up the human race. He maintains his patience and withholds his hand, waiting for us to respond properly to the word and Spirit of Christ. Our poor, mistaken, sin-ridden, faltering prayers come to the Almighty filtered "through Jesus Christ, our Lord." Jesus makes the most of what is worthwhile in them, and wisely screens out the rest. Something of his own Spirit gets into our prayers as he prays them for us. We certainly have a friend to speak for us at the court of heaven. If he were not there in glory upholding our cause, our days of grace would long since have run out, and history would have come to an earlier end in the last judgment.

from thence he shall come to judge . . .

What I have described as Christ's ascension was really the story of how God brought his Son back out of this perishing world and saved him from dying away like the rest of it. But Jesus' life had become entangled with other lives, for life does become involved with life as we interpenetrate and influence one another in many ways. It was as impossible to separate Jesus from other lives as it is to separate a plant from the soil, water, and air in which it grew. These things are taken up right into the plant's tissues. They are in the plant as much as the plant is in them. If Christ's word and Spirit have become a vital part of any man's life, all of Christ cannot be saved out of this world without taking something of that man along, too. We are raised together with Christ. Where he is, there we shall be also. The process of sorting out what is of Christ in this world's history is what is meant by the "judgment."

Christ has already passed through God's judgment and God was well pleased with him. Christ knows those lives that have been open to him. He knows what is his in the world. Who would make a better judge of all? In whom could I have greater confidence than in this one of us who is so much wiser than us all, with ages of experience? He himself had to master our kind of life. Christ understands us men from the inside, both as our maker and as one of us. This judge is the one who loved us so much that he made his painful way through the pounding waves of this world to rescue us from destruction in the cosmic undertow. He fought for us and he still wants us. I'm glad *he* is the one who is to be our judge.

Christ will discover and bring out to eternal safety, harmony, and usefulness whatever his Spirit has touched and been worked into. Saved history will include everything that was part of Christ's existence and doings. Something like this will have to happen: the Lord will bring our lives back out of the past and scan them as one reviews an old talkie film. He will run through the whole story of my life. Every moment that I have ever lived has been caught by God's candid camera. There will be a playback of everything I ever thought and said, openly or in secret. This is one show that I'm not very anxious to see, even if I myself play the starring role! Lord, have mercy! I hope that at least some parts of the chronicle of my life do feature Christ as the dominant influence over me. When the judge edits my documentary, he'll have to clip out an awful lot of waste film and dispose of it. How much of it will he save as part of his total story for the great festival? His judgment on every part will be final, correct, and absolute. Everything Christ has shaped will be caught up into the eternal future. I'm sure that nothing that had him in it will ever be lost. He is the Way, the Truth, and the Life. No man comes unto the Father but by him. If the Spirit of Christ is not in what

I'm doing, I'm wasting my life. Only what is built upon the rock of Christ will not be swept away by the flood when God's pent-up judgment bursts its dam. Non-Christian living is a slow process of suicide. Christ's truth is a boomerang that I may throw away, but it will come back and deal with me in the end. Christ is inescapable. I'm always on candid camera! This minute is certainly my last opportunity to live this minute in the Spirit of Christ.

. . . he shall come to judge the quick and the dead

Men who have heard Jesus' teaching often have serious doubts about whether a long-suffering life of love and truth will really win out in the end. So often it seems that the ruthless, deceitful, worldly powerful kind of man is the successful man. When Jesus comes out from his present hiddenness to judge the living (the quick) and the dead, it will settle the whole question about ultimate success directly and effectively. That day will see the greatest market crash of all time! The stock of all the goods and goals that most men chase after will go off the market when Christ is the only buyer. Some of the most "successful" will lose everything! But many who clung to Jesus faithfully throughout the long years, heartsick with waiting, will burst into rejoicing when they learn that their trust was not in vain. When the final assessment has been made, the only things that will be worth anything will be those that Christ values and that he had a hand in creating. My faith in Christ's final coming and judgment is my refusal to surrender the future to any other lord but Jesus Christ. Christ's values will be backed up by his God and Father, the ultimate power in the universe. I believe that God will break into history on a worldwide scale to vindicate Christ's way and decide human destinies.

Until he openly takes over this world, I'm responsible for doing what I can to heal and help the lives that the Lord lays before me. While I wait for his coming, the relief of men's urgent distresses must not be kept waiting. I mustn't be so rapt in looking for Christ coming on the clouds of heaven that I miss seeing him in "the least of these" who are in need around me. My ear must not be so set for the last trumpet that I don't hear the man who is standing next to me. I must not hold myself aloof from the affairs of men and history, believing in advance that the world is doomed. I'm not the judge. Christ is. God has sent me to bring Christ's word into the human problems of life, into men's jobs and culture. I must stake Christ's claim in all of life, for this world is the seed of the world to come.

I distrust any man who claims to know overmuch about the coming of Christ the Judge. The best minds were unable to describe the first coming of Christ in advance. How then can anyone spell out the manner of his second coming? The rich figurative words in which the Bible speaks of the last days may be interpreted in many profound ways. I must never insist that *I* have the only correct interpretation. Whatever I believe about these things must be flexible enough to allow for the freedom of God to do things, as he usually does them, in the most surprising ways. But I must never forget that the biblical pictures do point to some great forth-coming reality. While I don't know in detail the way future history will go, I do know that Jesus Christ is the only future of the past and present. I do believe that Jesus Christ gives to all things their final value and meaning, and that between him and ourselves there will someday be a final evaluating meeting.

I believe in the Holy Ghost

Before I go on with the third paragraph of the Creed, it's time for a glance back over the path we have followed. The story all arose out of the glorious unity of God the Father-Son-Holy Ghost in holy love. That interpersonal love was so utterly wonderful that there ought to be more and more of it. So God set out to build a creaturely world which would be like a hall of mirrors, reflecting the image, the glory of his love, in all directions.

First he prepared an array of amazing substances which could be put together in no end of ways with the most surprising results. Through millions of years God was working up his simplest materials into higher and higher forms of unity and coherence, moving toward a whole world that would reflect perfectly the image of his love. The dust of the earth was being called upward through the lesser creatures to make the human race within which Jesus Christ appeared. In this man's life God saw himself shining out clearly in the creaturely world for the first time. With such a start he could begin to build a human race which would bear his image in a new and corporate way. Imagine mankind with every man like Christ in attitude and behavior toward God and other men! How glorious! But what a God-sized task!

The church in its broadest and deepest sense was to be the next stage of God's world-building project. The people, the pattern, and the power were available. The power to bring it about? That's where the Holy Spirit comes in. And that's where I come in, with my pen in my hand. I believe that the Holy Spirit is using me right now as part of the process which is producing his church in his world, bringing his creatures toward their highest destiny.

God in his totality is involved, of course, in every one of his acts. But the three persons of the Holy Trinity may be distinguished helpfully by functions. God the Father-Creator brings things and people into existence, building into them all sorts of possibilities

God's Word, his eternal Son, calls people, and places them where they can use their possibilities to further God's purposes. But it is the special concern of God the Holy Ghost to awaken these possibilities, to bring hidden assets out into action, and to free men for their highest functions. The life of Simon, son of Jonas, shows the threefold role of God. Created by the Father, God's Son called Simon to forgiveness, discipleship, and apostleship, redirecting his life and renaming him Peter. But it was the Holy Spirit who set him on fire and brought everything that was in him out into such glorious service in the church that he will never be forgotten.

The Holy Spirit, then, is God working as development agent, as production manager, promotion director, expediter, and the like. He is God making the most of what he's got, moving all of us on the upward way toward our ultimate destiny in the fullness of Christ. The symbols of the Holy Spirit are those which show power moving in a definite direction. He is a wind, a bird in flight, a flowing stream, a flame burning upward and outward.

I believe in the Holy Ghost

The Holy Ghost reveals himself by what he has done. He works as silently as the June sunshine when it is growing grass, as invisibly as a magnet. I can detect him in my own life as he moves me out about my Father's business, to do what I was always meant to do. When someone rushes past my tableful of papers, the whoosh of wind blows the papers around and lands some of them on the floor. Even if I didn't *see* anybody, I would know that someone had passed by, because of the look of the papers. When God the Holy Ghost moves purposefully through this world, things move along with him, going his way. When my thoughts begin turning toward doing the kind of things Christ would have done, the Holy Spirit is at work.

In the beginning, when the Spirit of God moved over the face of creation, the waters brought forth their creatures, and the earth brought forth plants yielding fruit. By the Spirit men have always been moved to have fuller being. From the climate, the land, its bacteria, vegetation, indeed everything around us and in our history, the Spirit has unfolded the constructive possibilities which God built into the world and human life. He has always used *some* men to bring out the best that is in other men. Through inventors, artists, craftsmen, scientists, leaders, and the like, he brought the world's cultures and civilizations into being, with all that is worthwhile in human history. It was because the Hebrew prophets were enabled to discern God on the move in the story of their nation and the world that the Scriptures were written. By the Spirit Israel's history and leaders became a fitting cradle for the coming of Christ.

117

The Holy Spirit's greatest triumph was the life of Jesus Christ. By a special visitation of the Spirit, a maiden named Mary was enabled to conceive Jesus in her virgin womb. Attended by the Spirit, Jesus grew in wisdom and stature and in favor with God and man. By the Spirit he was designated as the one to bring men the good news of their liberation from sin and death, a liberation which he personally made possible by his own life and death in perfect truth and love. No man was ever so responsive to the touch of the Spirit as was Jesus. This was the secret of the power of his words and person. By the Spirit men were drawn to him and made whole. But for the world's sake the Spirit, who ordinarily aims to exalt all men, had to stand by and turn away as Jesus was humiliated, crucified, descending to the very depths of death. By the Spirit, however, Jesus was raised from death and hell to become the means of raising the rest of men to eternal life.

Through Jesus the Holy Spirit came to dwell in men. In Jesus' wonderful love for men God recognized an earthly counterpart of that divine love which unites the Holy Trinity. Jesus' love toward God was perfect. His human nature could therefore be exalted safely and expanded unimaginably, taken right into heaven and filled forever with all the fullness of God. This unreserved coming together of God and man in the ascended Lord made possible a wonderful new development. Till then the Holy Spirit had worked upon men more or less externally. The results, though sometimes spectacular, had always been quite temporary. But now that God was totally at one with the human nature of Jesus, the Holy Spirit could dwell within human beings permanently and eternally.

I believe in the Holy Ghost

Although Christ had ascended, something of him was still upon the earth: His words and the impact of his life were still affecting the lives of his followers. The Holy Spirit could pour through the heavenly Jesus into every life where Jesus' word had lodged. The ascended Jesus had become, as it were, the big end of a funnel whereby the Holy Spirit could enter the human race in depth, wherever Jesus' word came and was received. Jesus was like a transformer, stepping down the powers of the Creator Spirit so that he might come to dwell in men and bless them rather than burn them. On the day of Pentecost, therefore, the church came alive as a powerful, contagious, permanent community of holy love. The first Christians identified the source of their new life as the Spirit of Christ himself. They felt that their former Master, now their Lord, was again present with them, even in them, as the Holy Spirit. Some Christians refer to the "Holy Spirit" after Pentecost as the "Holy Ghost." This is because the word "ghost" is a far more human and personal word than the vaguer word "spirit," which somehow includes nonpersonal activity and force. A "ghost," whatever else it may mean, at least refers to the presence of some person who is bodily absent. Sensitive people understand presence. When Christians spoke Christ's word, there was a big stir among their hearers, just as when Jesus had been with them. The power of his Holy Ghost accompanied the least word-fragment of Jesus' life. Wonderful things happened in human lives as Christ's eternal life came into them. Looking ahead, Christians could see that a new, Christlike humanity could now arise, fulfilling the eternal purpose of the Christlike God who said, "Let us make man in our image, after our likeness."

The Holy Ghost makes the past of Christ present to me. If it were not for the Holy Ghost, Jesus' coming to the world would mean no more to me now than the life of any other great man. Anything he might have been or done in the distant past could not affect me. But through the Holy Ghost, my living contemporary, what Jesus was and obtained for me can come right through to me today, a direct connection. I can have at least a good taste of eternal life right now. Christ and all his benefits are really present to believers today. We are so united to Jesus by his Holy Ghost that we share in his baptism; we can live again something of his life of loving service; we can participate in his victory over temptation. While it is true that we shall share in something of Jesus' sufferings, we also share in his death-proof life. Jesus has already died for us those deeper passages of death which lie beyond the moment of our earthly death. We are being raised in his resurrection, ascending in his ascension. We have as yet only a fore-taste of these realities, but someday we shall come into the fullness of what is actually ours. Until then, the Holy Ghost will provide for us a continuous supply of resources for living, right from our Lord's overflowing spring.

I believe in the Holy Ghost

Man after man might tell me of all that Christ did for the world, but without the Holy Ghost it wouldn't mean a thing to me personally. The Holy Ghost makes me want to be free of everything that is hindering me from having fullness of life in the Lord. The Holy Ghost enables me to take God's side against everything in me that holds me back from my true destiny in Christ. The Holy Ghost gave me the gift of faith, so that I could really commit myself to Jesus Christ as my Savior and my Lord. The Holy Ghost has been steadily working in my life, striving to bring out the image of Christ's love and truth in me. The Holy Ghost is my Christian conscience, giving me a sense of responsibility for the total welfare of other people.

He imparts to me a love that reaches out toward the unloved and unlovely, creating new Christian fellowship. He makes prayer seem real and meaningful to me. He causes new light to flash out from the life and

words of Jesus, leading me ever deeper into the truth
of Christ, putting me up to doing the kinds of things
that Jesus did. As the Holy Ghost prompted the first
Christians to write out what they had to say about
Christ in the New Testament, so he impels me today
to write out what Jesus Christ means to me. I believe
that the Holy Ghost moved in the men who worked
out the Apostles' Creed, and that it is he who makes
their words live for me today.

By the Holy Ghost the church has become the
earthly future of Jesus Christ until the end of the age.
The Holy Ghost draws men together to form this new
body of Christ. He develops their several abilities for
the benefit of all, and convinces them that they must
use what they have in continuing the Lord's work
among men. Christ is depending on us to bring what
he began to its successful conclusion. He has no other
plans. If present-day churches refuse to move satisfactorily toward the unity and well-being of mankind,
then he will have to leave us to one side and, by his
Spirit, raise up another and more obedient people.
But no matter what becomes of us, the Lord will see
that his dream comes true. I believe in the Holy
Ghost! It is because I believe in the Holy Ghost that
I believe in the church. His specific aim is to develop
the church to its most glorious fullness. He seeks to
bring mankind into a Godlike unity of holy love, when
men will bear the image of God, not only one by one,
but all together. One solitary human being is not
enough to reflect the *whole* image of God, for God is

three as well as one. It takes at least two or three gathered together, at one with each other in a special way. God has never been content to develop individual men, however excellent. Throughout history he has always been working toward his kind of society. He set up his universe to produce nothing less than a great family and its eternal home—hence the church.

the holy catholic church

I couldn't have become a Christian without the church. The word of Christ had to come to me through churchmen. How much I owe to my wonderful church friends! The New Testament was written and translated for me by churchmen. Even the prayer our Lord taught us is cast in the plural: *Our* Father, give *us* this day *our* daily bread; forgive *us;* deliver *us.* Christ's command to preach points to a gathering of listeners. Baptism and the Lord's Supper involve the church family. Without the others I cannot fulfill Christ's command to love and take responsibility for others. I may be individually accountable to God. But as a member of God's family I will certainly have to give account of my relationship with the rest of his family. I can't be a Christian writer and yet bypass entirely what the church's great thinkers, councils, creeds, and confessions of faith have said. I couldn't be a Christian without the church anymore than I could be a soldier without an army, or a brother without a family.

I believe in the church, even though it is sometimes hard to distinguish from the rest of the world. My fellow Christians are undoubtedly an ordinary, even "ornery," lot of people. They have some of *my* human failings plus some of their own. Each congregation usually has its quota of tedious old men, fussy old women, distracted parents, rebellious young people, and thoughtless children. Any resemblance between what they are in church and what they are during the rest of the week is often purely coincidental. They seem to be forever struggling with problems and with one another. One group of them lives and worships in one style, while others do it differently. Where, in all the ordinariness, contrariness, and division, can I find God's church? Yet I believe it is there. The Holy Spirit is working in these people as well as in me. Something in me holds out its arms to something in them and also to Christ. Tarnished silver is still silver. These earthen vessels do contain the precious treasure of God. Christ came to join himself to problem people. He had to die for me, too, so I belong with the rest of those whom he has claimed for his own. In a way I'm glad the church isn't perfect yet. I would feel so out of place in a perfect church. They mightn't want to have me! But since there are already some hypocrites in the church, they are ready to take me in with the rest. *Everybody* in this world is a bit of a hypocrite anyway! Some of us admit it and come together at church to seek the Lord's mercy and renewal.

I believe in the church because I believe that God can finish what he began in Jesus' work. The church has not yet become what it will be. Church people have not yet arrived at their goal. But they are definitely on their way toward what the Lord would have them become. The meaning of their present condition will only be seen clearly when they reach the fulfillment that lies ahead of them. The church is by no means yet a showcase of polished specimens or a parade of crack troops shining in moral goodness. It is more like a hospital where people seek help. Thank you, Lord, for the help.

the holy catholic church

Many will probably turn away from the church because of me and my Christian friends, for sometimes we don't seem much like the "body of Christ." If I had been there when Jesus' dead, bruised, and broken body came down from the cross, I wouldn't have expected anything much from it. Yet that body, because it was Christ's, was transformed by God into the very means of rescuing all men from death. God can also do great things with Christ's new body, his church.

I believe in the church because it belongs to the

Lord. The church is composed of Jesus Christ and all those people in whom his word and Spirit are at work, together with their children, their property, and all of their influence in the world. No one but God can say for sure who or what is in or out of his church. "The Lord knoweth them that are his." But those who welcome Christ's word, who yield to his Spirit and show some of the fruits of his truth and love, recognize one another the world over. They belong together because they belong to the Christ who is in each of them. He draws them together with his own mysterious attraction. The church grows up around Christ and because of Christ. The church did not arise because some people with good intentions banded themselves together to promote what they considered to be a "good cause." Various clubs and associations may start that way. But the church originated in the eternal purpose of God, and it came into being because the Son of God came to this world and joined himself forever to as many as received his word and Spirit. No other society in the world has ever known the church's unique kind of togetherness. There is nothing in any of the world's religions that is the same kind of thing as the Christian church.

The church continues Christ's work. The church is that community of people in whom something of Jesus Christ still lives and moves on this earth, speaking his words and working his works. It is his new body by which the Lord continues to enter human history, touching men's lives wherever Christians go. He is

glad when other religions, heretical groups, governments, and humanitarian organizations also take up
his work of healing and feeding, helping and teaching.
Even though they don't give Christ the credit which
they owe him, at least his work is being done.

Churchmen must make Christ's word relevant to
their times. His truth and love have got to get through
to men, even though the church may have to change
some of its old ways of saying and doing things. Christ
has given abundant gifts to the members of his church,
and he expects proper arrangements to be made so
that those gifts will be available for those who need
them. There will therefore always be some kind of
church government, organization, and order. But the
organization must never come to exist for its own sake,
or lord it over all men, or presume to tell the Lord
what he may or may not do. If the church ever comes
to serve purposes that are merely humanly "useful,"
it begins at that point to fall short of Christ's purpose
for it. It is Christ's church. It is not the tool of parents,
communities, nations, or systems. The church must
always insist on being free enough to serve Christ's
purposes.

the holy catholic church

I believe in the church catholic. I must never let
any group of Christians walk off with this strong, won-

derful word "catholic" as if it were their peculiar property. This word means "according to the whole," that is, "the universal" church—all people where Christ is at work. If anybody were to ask me if I am catholic, I would answer, "Yes." Insofar as a Christian is truly a Christian, he is catholic, even though he may never have heard of Rome. Anyone who belongs to Christ belongs to the whole of Christ. To me the word catholic suggests the whole task of the whole church to bring the whole world to the whole Christ, making his love and truth so real that the whole life of all mankind may come to fulfill the whole purpose of God forever. This word catholic is a *big* word which speaks of inclusiveness and unity and repudiates all narrow littleness and divisiveness.

I believe that the church is holy because it belongs to the Holy One. His holiness is his godhood, his uniqueness, his whole difference as Creator from any of his creatures. When God's creatures are swept aside from their own little purposes and put into action for his specific holy purposes, they take on something of his holiness, however ordinary they may otherwise be. A holy one, or saint, is being separated from ungodly things and separated for God. This is like cleansing, which separates something *from* dirt and *for* usefulness. The church is the holy carrier of Christ's truth, love, and life. It is "separated unto the gospel." Its business is to be about Christ's business. Christlike things may be expected from Christ's holy church. It must be a distributing center for true peace and harmony, true reconciliation and unity among men. All the while it must also keep up a steady pressure against what is false, unloving, and un-Christlike. But it can only do this by being where men are, sharing their lot, and participating with them in the ongoing life of the world.

I believe that the holy catholic church is one church. Its unity centers in Christ who, in joining each member to God, joins him to every other member. The church's unity cannot be created by men. Unfortunately men have sometimes taken their different gifts from God and turned these diversities into divisions within the church. What a baffling variety of structures have been built on the one great foundation of Jesus Christ! We could rejoice in all this abundance if men didn't proceed to "unchurch" one another because of it, cutting themselves off from their brothers in Christ. When they do this, they are breaking the Lord's body, crucifying Christ afresh, afflicting him with groanings that cannot be uttered. But men cannot really tear the church asunder. The reality of the church's unity lies in its Lord, not in the hands of men. Brothers who quarrel and become estranged neither created their own brotherly connection in the first place, nor can they destroy this permanent family bond. Churchmen who are at odds with one another are sure to feel guilty, for Christ in them is wrestling with their human hostilities. When Christians disagree, they must always at least be willing to come together to seek new light from Christ and his forgiving mercy.

the communion of saints

A saint is a person quite ordinary in many ways, in whom Christ is at work. As such he shares in something of Christ's holiness, even though he is by no means perfected. Christ is committed to loving and rescuing him, as a man is committed to caring for his bride. We saints have many things in common. We have all responded to the upward calling of the Holy Ghost. We therefore understand things which some others cannot know. We all have the same task—bringing men out of unreality, isolation, and helplessness. Spiritual riches have accumulated from age to age as men responded to Christ, and this is the inheritance of all the saints. We share in the family tradition of Abraham, Moses, and Amos, Peter, John, and Paul. We join together in worship, fellowship, and service, with great mutual expectations. All this and much more is possible because each of us is in Christ and Christ in each. We love one another with the love of the great Lover who lives and loves in us all. Jesus Christ is the bond which creates the communion of saints.

The church, the communion of saints, is forever. These loving lives are bound together in Christ for all eternity. Neither the breadth of the earth nor the length of the years, the depth of the grave nor the height of heaven, will be able to separate us from

Christ, or from our loved ones in the Lord. Christ will always join us together whether in this world or some other. The sharp edge is taken off all our sad partings, because the eternal Christ is the eternal reality of the communion of saints. In him there can be no real division between the saints on earth and the saints in paradise. We are all one church forever in Christ Jesus our Lord. No power on earth can ever cut off the body of Christ on earth from its head and the rest of its members. The body of Christ may be floundering in deep waters, but its Head is safely above the flood. When all the families and tribes, clubs and nations have gone, the church will still remain.

If I believe in the communion of saints, I must show it in all my relationships with living Christians. We are channels of the water of life to one another. There is a priesthood of all believers. I need them and they need me. One burning coal separated from the others in the fire soon grows cold and loses its glow. I must share with the others the gifts and experiences which God has given to me. They should come to know the theology, history, and ways which I have inherited through my line of the church. And I must be willing to receive from other lines something of their inheritance, too. Anything that separates me from my brothers in Christ cannot be entirely right.

Because I believe in the church, I have joined it. I not only approve of there being a church—I have thrown my weight behind it! I have declared publicly my esteem for Christ and for the most Christlike souls who ever lived. I'm betting my life on Christ and his church. If I believe in the church, I must *be* the church wherever I am—at work, at play, at home, away. The Lord has promised to be with such people always, and I want nothing more.

the forgiveness of sins

God has a plan for his world, but that plan is always suffering setbacks because of things that people do and don't do. Some men may sin spectacularly, wrecking God's world and unleashing havoc on their fellowmen. Ordinarily we make trouble mostly by dealing with people deceitfully and handling them lovelessly. A sin is any kind of living that is foreign to the Spirit of Jesus Christ. It is any kind of action or inaction that hinders communion between man and man, or man and God. Sometimes I have had opportunities to take real steps forward toward God's goal—the communion of all men in holy love. But instead of building up good relations between people, I have sometimes set up tensions, distances, and strained relations.

Some of the currents of life are moving God's way and others aren't. I haven't always taken God's side and gone along with him. Instead I have actually gone along with, even helped, whatever is trying to tear down what God has been trying to build up. I have resisted the Holy Spirit's efforts to get me more deeply involved with other people's lives for Christ's sake. This kind of thing that hurts and holds back God, other people, and myself is sin. Even if I whitewash my sins with nice respectable names like mistakes, sickness, or unfortunate lapses, nevertheless I have sinned. I find that I can excuse myself for doing just about anything, or not doing it. When I'm through with the snow job, what I did doesn't sound like sin at all. I can blame somebody else, try to forget it, hide it, deny it, or make out that it's really only a trivial matter. But nevertheless I know that things are just not right between God and me and my fellowman. Something down deep inside me festers like the root of a forgotten tooth and spreads its poison throughout my whole life. Something ticks away down in there like a time bomb that sooner or later is going to wreck me. My sin has got to be dealt with somehow, neutralized and deactivated.

It's strange how sin usually looks like the smart thing to do until somebody's done it. Sin is so fascinating that often people eagerly seek it. But afterward, when they're running away, it bumps along after them. It's now a part of their life. What has been done has been done, and it will have devastating effects on more and more people. Many a life will be crushed in the path of the avalanches of misery that have been started by seemingly simple sins.

But surely *I* have never done anything terrible? What did *I* ever do to hurt anybody? I should ask,

What have I *not* done to help people? I just lived for myself in a world of lost, miserable folk who were left to die, unloved and alone. I just ate my regular three meals a day and slept peacefully, while over half the world went to bed hungry. I have just put my feet up, read in the paper about a world full of tortured souls, then yawned unconcerned and nodded off. Maybe my idea of a good life is a horrible nightmare to God! How many people are suffering just now because of something I didn't do that I might have done? Lord, forgive me my debts as well as my trespasses!

the forgiveness of sins

When I find that I can own up to my sins, Christ's truth has got through to me at last. When I have become concerned about my sins, Christ must be there and at work within me. Christ in me not only convinces me that I am in the wrong but enables me to admit it to others. He also makes me want to set things right. When I realize that Christ is moving there within me, I know that God has not cast me off entirely. He is not only judging me, he is saving me through Christ. God is not holding my sins against me. If he has not allowed my sins to stand between him and me, that must mean that he has forgiven me. Two people in each other's arms are certainly not quarreling. Once I realize God has forgiven me, I must accept his forgiveness and forgive myself.

By the Spirit of Christ a new kind of living keeps on appearing in me. In the place of the old self-centered ways, Christ gives me *his* ways. *For* the old, he *gives* the new. This is for-giveness.

What is of Christ in me belongs to God forever. For the sake of what is Christlike in me, God puts up with the rest of my living. He accepts me and hopefully goes on working with me, even though he doesn't approve of what I have been and done. This too is forgiveness of sins.

Maybe God can use even the bad scenes in my life, turning them somehow, someday, into some kind of good. Blotches on an artist's canvas can often be worked usefully into the final painting. God may be able to resolve my awful discords into enriched harmonies. When an ugly rock is covered by white foam, rainbow spray, and sparkling reflections, it can become a thing of beauty. When my sins have been surrounded by the life of Christ, even the darker parts of my life may be transformed into an unexpected glory. This would indeed be a marvelous forgiveness of my sins.

As for the effects of my sins on other lives, God has put his church into the world to do what it can to repair that kind of damage. As the church helps those who are in distress because of other people's sins, I see God's forgiveness at work, absorbing sin. The deadly force of every sin, whomever it affects throughout its career of misery, is ultimately spent on the suffering heart of God.

I believe in forgiving sins against myself. Otherwise I wouldn't dare ask God in the Lord's Prayer to forgive me in the same way I forgive others. My family must learn how to forgive sins against our family circle and accept the offenders, hoping all things for them in Christ. In the same way the church family has to learn to forgive members who have made trouble for the church family. This churchly forgiveness may be expressed by an official of the church in a special ceremony, but it is useless unless the other members open their hearts to the sinner who has been restored to the communion. But all sins against myself, against my family, against the church and all others, involve an element of sin against God. God alone can forgive the sin against God. God reaches out through his church, offering men his forgiveness through Christ. The church is, at its best, God's forgiveness in search of those who need it.

the resurrection of the body

My *physical* body is important to God. He created me with this body and expected me to do what I could with it for his purposes. He went to a lot of trouble to build and maintain this body which makes me a part of nature, history, and human society. My body has certainly been important to me. In it, by it, and with it I live and have my being—and write this book.

Death is the ultimate enemy for me as for all God's creatures. Death threatens every moment of our perishing existence. Dying is no mere illusion, nor is it a welcome release from prison. Otherwise Jesus would not have agonized so in Gethsemane. Death means business—or rather, the end of all business. It puts a stop to whatever we are doing, puts an end to the possibilities of people growing closer together in this world. The deepest tragedy of death lies in the disruption of love.

"My body" doesn't mean merely my flesh, blood, and bones. It means all that I am as a creature and a person, as in the words "somebody, anybody, everybody." It also means all that I have been and done from birth to death, the whole stir I made in the world. Body means me, including my organism. Resurrection of the body doesn't mean my corpse simply coming alive again. Nor does it imply that, when I have risen, my old kind of life will continue as usual. There will be most unusual alterations! Resurrection means that God will take all of me that has ever been, and so deal with me that I shall be somehow as Jesus is now. He will completely fulfill this life I have lived. I don't know how he will work this transformation. He made my body once, out of dead stuff eaten as food, and I'm sure he can do it again. What I have been is maybe a kind of seed which he can use in growing some unimaginable new kind of body. What I shall be won't be merely what I am now, but it will certainly be continuous with what I am now. A full-grown plant is continuous with the seed from which it came, though it is quite different from the seed.

Resurrection of the body means that God has an eternal use for creatureliness, nature, time and space, history, individuality, and all our helpful earthly labors. It means that my world and I not only have a meaning now, but also a goal ahead.

I believe in the resurrection of the body because I believe that Christ is the Lord of all things. All bodily life that rejected Christ will be confronted by its Judge and a cosmic garbage dump. All bodily life that acted in the Spirit of Christ will be preserved forever as his body. Only the Lord knows how much of this world he considers his body to be.

When our *earthly* life first enters the risen and rising body of Christ, a healing wholeness begins immediately to repair sin's ravages on our health, our homes, and society in general. Our fully risen bodies will truly and fully express what we are already becoming in Christ. We shall be free to serve God and enjoy him and our loved ones in the Lord forever. A blessed reunion with dear ones, still themselves, but delivered from their handicaps and faults! A clear understanding of what the world's story was all about! The answers to umpteen questions, and a whole perfected universe to explore! I don't want to miss the resurrection of the body, and— in Christ—I won't.

and the life everlasting

I believe in life. Life is no dream or passing fancy. Life is not a calamity from which I want to be delivered. My life can, however, be so dragged down to ill health, failure, and sin, that I wouldn't particularly want to have to go on and on living this plagued kind of existence. Living forever could be hell unless everlasting life is a life of the highest type, including memory, understanding, ability, joy, love, and hope for more of the same forever and ever. I believe that our Lord is living this kind of life right now. His life is the only eternal life there is. The good news is that *we* can share in this Christ-life, both in its kind and its duration. He has made his life available for us. He offers it to us and makes it possible for his kind of life to begin even in these earthly lives that we now live. The life that triumphed in him will bring us to triumph as well. Oh glorious, glorious gift!

Life everlasting will not be stagnation. We shall not be frozen into one unmoving, permanent tableau or fixed forever at our present stage of development. The panorama of the endless possibilities ahead of us cannot be described by our little guesses. We are the only creatures God ever made which do not attain full development in one life span. Away ahead of us will stretch unimaginable vistas of unlimited development as we serve

139

God's purposes gladly without haste or waste. What each one of us needs for his perfection will be available to us. There will be lots of "time" to finish all our beginnings.

Christ will be there. That's how *we* get to be there—because of his eternal life in us. We shall see him as he is and understand what he meant when he said, "I am the resurrection and the life." *Jesus Christ is the life everlasting.* This last phrase of the Creed is full of Christ, and it is the Creed's pinnacle point. Looking through the veil of these words, I see Christ standing in glorious union with all of us who have come to him. He who was in the plan from the beginning stands there as the end and the goal of the whole story of God's world: God with man forever. With God the Creed began—and it ends likewise with God. His was and is and evermore will be the power and the glory.

Through Christ he has dealt with all three of our ultimate enemies, death, sin, and the grave. There will be no more dying in the life everlasting. We who have received Christ's gift of eternal life shall be safe from the destroyer forever. Though today my head may hang with shame because of my sins, in the life everlasting they will be no more remembered against me. God will be able to trust me as fully as he trusts his only begotten Son. Though today I mourn because some of my richest joys and fairest hopes and dearest earthly loves lie buried in some graveyard, in the life everlasting I shall rejoice at Christ's power to restore what I had lost. He is the resurrection and the life. That not only means complete and final deliverance from the destroyer. It also means movement ever onward and upward from glory to glory until we are as closely at one with God as is the human side of Jesus. The gospel, the best news ever, is that the way to this life everlasting was opened to us by Christ. I believe in it from the bottom of my heart.

Amen

When I say the *amen* at the end of the Creed, it is really the third time I have said, "I believe." At the beginning I said, "I believe in God," then later, "I believe in the Holy Ghost." This little Hebrew word *amen* means, "So be it," or, "I agree with that," or, "That's what I sincerely believe." I'm glad there is an *amen* at the end of the Creed because I need some way of expressing my faith all at once in everything that the Creed says to me about Jesus Christ. I always say this last word firmly and triumphantly, for I really do believe in the God and the gospel I find in the Creed.

I believe in the Creed because I believe in Jesus Christ. There is something of him in every phase. Without him there is nothing to hold the church's teachings together—no string for the beads. He is the whole message we have to give to the world. We are to be witnesses identifying him as God's gift to man. Too often we have been pointing to everything else but Christ. I have found that people immediately argue with me when I talk to them about the church, about the Bible, the sacraments, the ministry, liturgy, theologies, denominations, even Christianity and Christendom. But not many quarrel with the life Christ lived. If we are saved by participating in his life rather than by accepting an interpretation of his life or of these other matters, we can stop arguing and start living as brothers. When church people center their thoughts, conversation, sermons, and services everywhere else but on Christ, we can only expect disintegration, disunity, and despair. Today many thinkers are calling for a new reformation. But any reformation which does something less than give Christ his proper central place will be merely a new variety of the oldest folly. To put Christ in the center of everything Christian would be such a novel and radical move that it might even raise the dead! The world might welcome the new emphasis much more than churchmen would. It's so hard to change our old ways, even if they are strangling us.

If my thoughts on the Creed help anyone to pull his thoughts and life together around Christ, I shall be glad. May voice after voice throughout the world join me in saying *Amen* to the Creed, which is Christ.

It is all too easy to wander away from Christ into all sorts of vague speculations about fringe matters. What about predestination? Who will be saved? What about the heathen and the other religions? It is also easy to become lost in struggling with the problems of our personal and social life. When we lose touch with Christ for whatever reason, our line goes dead. Our power cuts off and we can't move. In my dark hours, when I don't even feel like a Christian, the trouble is always that I have taken my eyes off Christ and turned to something else. I'm always thankful when we say the Creed at church, for then I'm brought back to the facts about Christ and my life begins again. No wonder I repeat the Creed with such relish and join so enthusiastically in saying *Amen*.